UNCOMFORTABLE EITHER WAY

www.amplifypublishinggroup.com

Uncomfortable Either Way: Why Choosing Easy Is Making Your Life Hard

©2025 Brett Eaton. All Rights Reserved. No part of this publication may be reproduced, stored in a retrieval system or transmitted in any form by any means electronic, mechanical, or photocopying, recording or otherwise without the permission of the author.

The advice and strategies found within may not be suitable for every situation. This work is sold with the understanding that neither the author nor the publisher is held responsible for the results accrued from the advice in this book.

For more information, please contact:
Amplify Publishing, an imprint of Amplify Publishing Group
620 Herndon Parkway, Suite 220
Herndon, VA 20170
info@amplifypublishing.com

Library of Congress Control Number: 2024923736

CPSIA Code: PRV0425A

ISBN-13: 979-8-89138-037-0

Printed in the United States

To my mom, dad, and beautiful wife—thank you for your love, patience, and encouragement.

To the person reading this who knows they are capable of a "richer," more fulfilling life . . . I'm here to tell you it's not only possible but incredibly rewarding. You just need to decide that you are worth it.

To my younger self—thank you for never giving up on your wild and crazy dreams, for recycling your deepest pain and using it to help others, and for writing the book I wish I could have read in my twenties.

BRETT EATON

UNCOMFORTABLE EITHER WAY

WHY CHOOSING EASY IS MAKING YOUR LIFE HARD

CONTENTS

PART IV: HOW TO AVOID THE "F*CK IT" BUTTON

PART V: EXPECT IT TO BE HARD

PART VI: WHAT'S YOUR NEXT UNCOMFORTABLE?

PROACTIVITY

If there's anything I've learned in fifteen years studying high performers, it's that people don't grow or discover our strengths when everything's cool and life is going great. It's when everything goes sideways that we learn who we really are.

Life taught me that the hard way, with two events that happened when I was just sixteen.

For many high school students, sophomore year is one of the most enjoyable and memorable. It was certainly memorable for me, but far from enjoyable. Actually, it was the worst year of my life. It also became the most impactful.

I was born in Bergen County, New Jersey, and raised in a great family. I had one sister, who was two and a half years older, and by all accounts, she was the smart one. Luckily for me, I found my identity in sports. By the time I was sixteen, I was a three-sport athlete—basketball, football, and baseball—at my high school. But in my sophomore year, I started having back pain, and my trainers and doctors couldn't figure out what was going on.

Once, I was playing shortstop, and the batter hit a pop-up into shallow left field. I went back and tried to do one of those over-the-shoulder catches like one of my idols, the great New York Yankees shortstop Derek Jeter, and . . . something gave in my lower back. It kind of hurt, and I could tell something was off, but I was young and bulletproof, so I didn't think too much of it. The next inning I went up to bat, and when I swung, the pain became so excruciating that I limped to first base. With every step it felt like somebody had stabbed me and left the knife in. What was happening?

My parents took me to a doctor, who said, "Okay, this is no big deal." Thinking it was just a pinched nerve or slight strain, I spent the next two weeks seeing both chiropractors and physical therapists, and two weeks later, with the pain having mostly subsided, I was back in the lineup again. But as soon as I swung the bat, tried to bend over, or did anything that required a twisting motion, the pain came back immediately and I was in agony. This went on for months.

My back got so bad that at one point I remember limping down the hallway at school, staring at the ground, tears running down my face. When I got to my Spanish class, my teacher took one look at my face and immediately called the nurse. This was more than a strain or pinched nerve. Finally, after months of physical therapy, orthopedic surgeons, and spinal adjustments with no relief, my doctor looked at my mother and me and said, "We have two options. We can surgically fuse his lumbar spine from L2 to L5, or we can wait a year, remove him from all sports, have him do physical therapy, and see if he grows out of it."

Spinal fusion surgery on a sixteen-year-old is a terrible idea. Forget it. But knowing what I know now about fitness, doing nothing for a year was also a terrible option.

If I had known then what I know now about fitness and anatomy, thanks to my Exercise Science degree and more than a decade in the fitness industry, I never would have agreed to sit on my ass for twelve months. But multiple doctors told me those were my options, so that was what I did. Three hundred and sixty-five days without sports. I missed my entire sophomore year of basketball and junior year of football and ended up having to give up baseball completely, which was devastating.

Sports were a huge part of who I was, and I had been counting on earning an athletic scholarship to a top university to take the financial stress off my parents. But universities usually make their scholarship decisions during junior year, and I was a no-name stuck on the sidelines.

Instead, I spent that year doing basic physical therapy twice a week while we waited for my back to magically heal itself. I hated this plan. It frustrated me daily, and it turned out to be the worst thing I could have done because I got dumpy, lazy, and out of shape. When I was finally cleared and returned to play quarterback as a senior, I saw how bad that advice had really been. I had to come back not only from a back injury but also from being the weakest and most deconditioned I've ever been. The difference was that this time, I changed my strategy.

Throughout that summer and the next year, my back injury would flare up here and there, but instead of shutting everything down and doing nothing, I got to work and did everything.

I lived in the weight room. I started taking chest-deep ice baths. I stretched. I continued to work with my physical therapist, except now it was me pushing them. I even took a summer job in construction so I could be moving, lifting, and on my feet all day. All of a sudden, muscle started to reappear. All of a sudden, my core was stronger. I was more flexible. I was moving my body like it was meant to move, and I felt so much better. If I could go back, I would say to my doctor, "Screw your year of sitting and waiting. Instead of doing therapy twice, let me do it four times a week. On top of that, put me in the gym with our school's athletic trainer. Let me work with somebody who's going to get me stronger and fitter and help me heal faster."

I can't share the story of my back injury without also sharing the second, and even harder, lesson I learned that came just two months after my back diagnosis. My sister was home from college for spring break, and we were all sitting around the table for a big family dinner. Rare for a Friday night. It was one of the best family dinners we ever had. Mom had made her specialty chicken, my dad got home from work in a great mood and was cracking jokes at the table, and everybody was laughing. It was beautiful. After it was over, I went off to my friend's house to watch a movie. We watched *8 Mile*, the story of rapper Eminem. I remember it like it was yesterday because I've still never seen the second half of that movie. About an hour after I arrived, the phone rang. My friend's mom asked me to come upstairs and said, "Brett, something's happened to your dad, and he's being rushed to the hospital."

Minutes later I was in the car with my friend's mom as she drove me to the hospital and tried to keep me calm. When we pulled up to the hospital, I sprinted to the front desk. But before I could get there, I turned left and immediately made eye contact with my mom and sister, who were at the far end of the long hallway. My mom was frantic and on the phone with tears in her eyes, and they both had that "devastated and barely keeping it together" look on their faces. As soon as they saw me, they both started sobbing.

I knew instantly that my biggest fear was confirmed: my dad was dead of a heart attack at fifty-two years old. It was April 23, 2003.

This shook my world because I thought my dad was invincible. Sure, he was heavier than he should have been, but he was my hero. How could this happen to my hero? He was one of those heavy athletic dads, but he was also funny, with a loud, contagious laugh that made him the life of any party. A guy people wanted to be around. Just like that, he was gone.

This was the kind of thing I'd see in movies or read in the news but never thought could actually happen to me and to my family. Overnight, I went from a sixteen-year-old teenager focused on getting back on the field to the man of the house, now responsible for my mom and my sister. All I wanted to do to deal with my grief was to immerse myself in sports and take my aggression and anger out in training and on my opponents, but I couldn't. I was still in physical pain and still being advised to remain on the sidelines and take it easy.

It was an incredibly difficult and frustrating time—the hardest I have ever experienced. I was pissed off and angry at everyone and everything. The word *depression* gets thrown around a lot these days, but that was as low a place as I've ever experienced.

TWO LIFE-ALTERING LESSONS

Those were terrible years by any measurement, but I also learned two incredible, life-changing lessons from that time.

First—life is meant to be played on offense.

Those early experiences really opened my eyes and showed me how many of us spend our whole lives playing defense. Playing by the rules, waiting for the right time, and working toward someone else's definition of success instead of prioritizing our own. It shouldn't take a catastrophic injury or the death of a loved one to motivate you to make positive changes in your life. But we procrastinate, rationalize, and make excuses, and then we wonder how ten years have flown by.

I'm here to shed light on why that happens—and, more importantly, to show you how you can get out of your own way, get moving, get growing, and start doing the things and making the impact you know you are capable of.

Instead of playing defense—sitting around and hoping my back would magically heal and my situation would change—I was proactive.

I do that in every part of my life now, and I encourage you to do the same. Don't wait for things to happen. Play offense.

The second lesson was that I was going to die.

We all know intellectually that we're going to die. We all know the clock is ticking; that's part of being human. But there's a deeper, scarier truth we don't like to think about: *we have no idea when it's going to happen.*

Unless you're very old, you probably dismiss death as being safely in your far future, and maybe it is. You might have decades in front of you, but you have no way of knowing that for sure. That means every day you spend stuck in neutral—talking about the things you'll do, the places you'll go, and the life you'll build "someday," while putting off doing anything about them—is a day wasted and increases the risk that time will run out and that you'll never accomplish any of those things. You'll be a cautionary tale, a "might have been." Because one day, you won't have any more *somedays*, and all you'll wish for then is that you had more time.

That doesn't even have to mean something as dramatic as a heart attack or getting hit by a bus. It doesn't have to mean the Grim Reaper tapping you on the shoulder at all. Maybe you develop a chronic, disabling illness. Maybe your parents decline sharply and only you can give them the care they need. Maybe you lose your job due to a layoff. *Boom*, like a lightning strike, priorities shift, and all these plans you had for tomorrow become regrets. Forget about starting your dream business or getting in the best shape of your life; now you're just surviving. Meanwhile, that clock is still ticking.

This is your time, right now, to embrace change, stop hitting the snooze button, get out of bed, and take steps toward creating the future you've been secretly fantasizing about. Eventually, if you don't choose, life chooses for you, without your permission and without mercy.

I don't want to see you crippled by regret. I don't want people at your funeral talking about all the things you "said you were going to do." I want them marveling over the courageous, brilliant, generous, crazy, joyful life that you led! But for that to happen, you have to do one thing right now, before you move to the next paragraph:

Stop lying to yourself about what you will do tomorrow.

Stop telling yourself you'll make big changes "someday" or "tomorrow." Because unless you change how you think and the choices you make, you'll keep saying that until you run out of tomorrows. That can happen in the blink of an eye.

It wasn't until years after my dad's death that I learned he had all kinds of things he wanted to do later in his life, but he never got to do them. After he died, I swore that I would never defer my biggest life goals and dreams by saying things such as "One of these days, I'm going to . . ." or "When the time is right, I'll . . ."

That's how I ended up moving to San Diego and then Florida after dreaming for years about living at the beach. That's how I became an entrepreneur and started working for myself. That's what drove me to finally write this book. That's how I started speaking and sharing this message. *Do it. Make it happen and start living a life that feels more aligned and fulfilling to you. Live your dreams now.* Because none of us really know how much time we have left.

WHAT YOU'LL GET OUT OF THIS BOOK

In my coaching work, I've discovered the two biggest mistakes all of us people make when trying to make big, important changes in our lives.

First, we rely on excitement and willpower instead of setting up systems and remaking our environment to make it easier to do the right things. Willpower is for suckers. It's great if you have it, but people who change their lives rely on willpower sparingly or not at all.

Second, we don't give enough credit to how our emotions influence our choices. We think we're rational beings doing things for logical reasons, but we're not. We want what we want, even if it's to chase the easy sale, eat that double-bacon cheeseburger simply because it smells good, or buy the new hot item on Amazon because we love seeing the package arrive at the door. But what we've become most addicted to is *staying comfortable*—to doing what's familiar and avoiding the inconvenience or embarrassment of changing our habits, looking like a beginner, pushing ourselves, or ending relationships we know are bad for us.

The truth at the heart of this book is this:

Choosing easy is making our lives harder.
It's our default for comfort that wastes our time
and potential and prevents us from feeling fulfilled.

If you want to rise above ordinary, stop saying "Someday" about your cherished goals, and become the version of you that you've always dreamed about being, you've got to understand your emotional need for comfort and how to overcome it.

That's what I'm going to do in this book. We're going to go on a journey of truth, with tough love, some humor, and massive hugs and hand-pounds at the end.

I won't be pulling any punches because my job isn't to keep you comfortable; it's to empower you. I'm going to help you break your addiction to excuses. I'm going to help you confront the self-delusions that keep you from seeing problems and moving forward. I'm going to show you the dangers of taking shortcuts because shortcuts skip to the end of the story without changing who you are.

I'm going to call you out on the myths you've been clinging to, the excuses that are destroying your confidence, and the bullshit lies you've been telling yourself. I'll help you confront your self-doubt, denial, shame, and fear. Most of all, I'm going to help you overcome your natural instinct to avoid discomfort and instead embrace it. If you can do that, you can achieve virtually anything.

My goal is to recalibrate and rewire how you think, speak, and act for the better—forever.

The ideas I'll be sharing are both relevant and applicable to any area of personal and professional high performance, including those of most common concern for my clients, such as the following:

- Fitness and weight
- Physical and mental health
- Career, business, and entrepreneurship
- Relationships
- Finance
- Life goals and experiences
- Joy and fulfillment

I despise things that are boring, so I'm going to make this journey enjoyable with some features you'll find in almost every chapter.

- **Calling Bullshit—**I'll call out myths most of us are being fed that are actually 100 percent pure American-made bullshit.
- **Uncomfortable Truths—**Together, we'll face some harsh realities that you won't enjoy being called out on but will be glad I did. If you can stomach the tough love, these will

rewire your approach and bring about major breakthroughs for you.

- **Momentum Builders—**Don't you hate books that make you wait until the last chapter for practical tips and a solution? Me too, which is why I struggle to finish them. My mission is not to motivate you; it's to help you build momentum. The coach in me can't allow you to read this book cover to cover without taking action and building confidence and momentum every step of the way. So at the end of each chapter, I'll give you two actions you can put to work right away. One you'll be able to do immediately, before you even turn the page, and the other you can do by the end of the day. Take these momentum-building actions seriously and watch your confidence and self-belief grow as you read.

I wish I could promise you that this book will change your life, but I can't, because no book alone can do that. What I will promise is this: If you take action TODAY (not "someday" or "tomorrow") on the techniques and strategies I teach you, *you* will change your life and it will be the most rewarding and fulfilling journey of your life.

Sound fair? Great, let's get started.

PART I

UNCOMFORT VS. DISCOMFORT

YOU'RE ALREADY UNCOMFORTABLE

It's Northern Virginia, 2014. I pull into a parking spot and sit in my car with the engine running. As I stare at the building where I'll spend the next ten hours, I'm once again overcome with dread and an anxious pit in my stomach. How many useless emails will I have to answer? How many pointless meetings will I have to stay awake through? Who's going to call in sick? How many times will I hear someone say, "Hey, Brett, do you have a minute?" One thing I know is that by the end of the day, I won't have accomplished anything I intended to when I got up that morning.

Even my personal workout has become a coin flip. There's a good chance I won't end up taking a lunch break, so the only opportunity I'll have to work out will be at 8:00 p.m., when my workday ends, and I'll probably be too exhausted. In fact, skipping my workout has become the rule, not the exception, these days.

Did I mention that at this point I was still working in the fitness industry?

Don't get me wrong; I liked being a fitness manager. I liked working with people. I liked helping them get in shape while improving their mindset and resilience. What I hated was all the administrative crap that took up so much of my time. I had no freedom or flexibility to do what I wanted. I was showing up at 7:00 a.m., leaving at 7:00 p.m., and barely making enough money to get by. I started to wonder, "Am I going to be doing this for the next thirty years? How many more years will this be my schedule? How will I ever have a wife or kids if I'm never home? And why the hell does it seem like all my friends are working less and making more money than I am?"

It wasn't just the hours. I felt like I was wasting my gifts. I'd always felt like I could help groups of people find motivation, build momentum, overcome barriers, and reach their goals beyond just fitness. But I wasn't able to do it in that job. I had all these great ideas I wanted to implement, but because we were a corporate location, those ideas kept getting shot down. Then in 2015 I had my "come to Jesus" moment. I was in the running for a promotion to regional director of fitness, and when I went in for the interview, I felt like I killed it. But when I got back to my car, I felt another overwhelming rush of anxiety. I said, "Shit, I actually hope I don't get the job." I would be driving more, crunching numbers, and doing nothing fitness-related. I would hate it. Why not just go to DC and work for a bank and make more money punching spreadsheets? That was the moment I said, "Whoa, I'm officially climbing a ladder I don't want to be on. Something needs to change."

I've already mentioned the idea of living life on offense versus defense. That means you're never standing still. You're either playing offense, actively growing and in control of your own life, or playing defense and hoping things will somehow change on their own without you having to actually change or work for them. When you play *not* to lose, you've already lost.

During those two years, I was the poster child for living life on defense. I was reactive, unprepared, stressed, overwhelmed, unmotivated, undisciplined, and, most of all, uninspired. That was when I started looking for motivation anywhere I could and quickly found myself down a rabbit hole: watching motivational speakers on YouTube. Something about the passionate energy with which they spoke, as well as their vibrant charisma, fascinated me. Then one fateful day, a friend sent me a link to a podcast called *The School of Greatness*, hosted by Lewis Howes. Listening to that one episode would turn out to be a sliding door moment for me. The host and his guest spent an hour discussing the reasons why routines and boundaries are critical for success and why success isn't random. Success is *planned.*

This seemingly simple yet profound idea stopped me in my tracks. I couldn't stop thinking about it. I hadn't been planning my success at all. I'd been sitting around hoping for it. I became obsessed with studying the most inspiring, successful, and fulfilled people in the world. How did they reach the level they were at? What did they do every day? What standards did they hold themselves to? What questions did they ask? How did they view money and grow wealth? How did they allocate their time? How did they speak to themselves and others? Who did they surround themselves with? How did they stay encouraged and build what seemed like unstoppable momentum?

Every morning for the next two years, I listened to a motivational video or podcast. I absorbed everything I could. I'd write things down that resonated and listen multiple times if it was a good one. Over time, a pattern emerged. I started to connect the dots to what drove those high achievers.

Want to know what it is? Are you ready?

They had a clear target, they had a game plan, and they played offense.

I know, right? That's it. The people who consistently got more done, who seemed to be working with a twenty-six-hour day when the rest of us only have twenty-four, planned out their time in exhaustive detail. They expected to have great days, to get a lot done, and to dominate, so they did.

At that moment I was forced to face an uncomfortable truth. There was no way I could ever make the impact I wanted to make or realize my potential if I stayed at my dead-end fitness manager job. But I didn't know what to do next. The idea of leaving without a soft place to land was terrifying. Desperate for change, I joined a multi-level marketing (MLM) company as my "side hustle." It was a great learning experience and opened me up to a new way of thinking about time and my future, but within about ten months, I knew it wasn't for me. I hated the idea of trying to sell products I wasn't deeply invested in to my friends and family. However, while I was still involved, I attended a conference with the other members. It blew my mind. Everyone was there for the same reason: to grow their business, think bigger, and learn how to get something more out of life. MLM didn't align with who I wanted to be, but I could feel myself falling in love with the personal growth industry. I needed to get around more people who weren't satisfied with mediocrity.

Shortly afterward, I felt called to attend another conference, this one led by Lewis Howes (the host of the podcast I mentioned earlier) called the "Summit of Greatness." That was the first time I said, "There's a whole world out there of personal growth information and people wanting to change everything!" The conference was eight hours away from where I lived, and because I was living paycheck to paycheck, I drove and stayed in the attic of the cheapest Airbnb I could find. The event set me on fire. On the drive home, I didn't turn the radio on once because my brain was going a hundred miles per hour. I was thinking, "Something needs to change for me, and it needs to change as quickly as possible."

I know what typically happens after conferences: people are all fired up for a week or two, but nothing really changes and they slide back into their old habits and routines. I had seen it with most of my team members after the MLM conference. I needed to prevent that from happening and knew I needed to take a big leap. I spent my last few dollars to buy my ticket for the following year's Summit and promised myself two things: One, I would not allow myself to go back unless I felt I made progress and earned the right to return the following year. Two, I had two weeks to make a bold change.

Two weeks later I swallowed my pride and demoted myself from fitness manager back to personal trainer, and while that took precious money out of my pocket, it gave me something more valuable at that moment: *time.* Four days a week, I trained clients for twelve hours a day. During the other three, I started learning everything I could about building a personal brand, starting a business, and becoming a high-performance coach.

I used my current fitness clients as guinea pigs. I developed my specific messaging and methods. I learned everything I could about finance, entrepreneurship, business, and more. I created my own planning process to escape my repetitive weekly funk of surviving until the weekend. I went back to the Summit of Greatness the next year, and when I came back, I was even more fired up. That was when I took an even bigger leap. I knew it was time to remove the safety net, so I gave my two weeks' notice. This scared the shit out of me, but the only way I would ever find out if I could make it working for myself was to try it without always having the gym as my Plan B.

That move changed my life. I adapted the planning process I was using for myself and started teaching it to my clients to help them stick to their workout and eating schedules, and it began to ripple positively across other areas of their lives. In a few years, I went from being a dead-end personal trainer to a passion-driven coach and strategist, helping hundreds of people create the habits, routines, and mindset they needed to squeeze every drop of success, vitality, and happiness out of life.

Finally, I was playing offense!

CALLING BULLSHIT

We look at ripped actors such as Chris "Thor" Hemsworth or billionaires such as Warren Buffett and assume they have some kind of superhuman muscle fibers or intellects. But they don't. In his landmark paper "The Mundanity of Excellence," researcher Daniel Chambliss found the following:

- **Excellence requires doing small, ordinary things consistently right.**
- **Innate talent is not responsible for high achievement.**
- **Significant improvement results from qualitative changes in deliberate practice of skills, not from doing more of the same.**

In other words, superheroes aren't born. They're made.

ADDICTED TO EASY

Sorry for the long story, but it's important that you know that not long ago, I was where you might be right now: stuck, unhappy, frustrated, and mad at yourself. So I get it. You're frustrated because you want more out of your life, you know there's more for the taking, and the only thing stopping you from taking it is *you*. Sound about right?

Your problem is that you're human. We're wired to seek comfort, abundance, and predictability. Ten thousand years ago, our ancestors lived as nomadic hunter-gatherers on the African veld, and their daily existence was precarious. They had no permanent homes. They ate what they could forage or kill (and what they hunted tended to fight back), so they were always near starvation. A storm, a plague, or an attack from another tribe was an extinction-level event. So when humans finally invented agriculture and cities, we said, "Wait, we can have walls to keep us safe and a steady supply of grain? Hell yeah!" and settled in. Eventually, we invented antibiotics, Uber Eats, and iPhones; put our feet up; and enjoyed finally being able to Netflix and chill.

There's just one problem with that. Being comfortable sends us signals that say, "Everything's cool. Nothing needs to change," and we listen. Comfort gives us what we want but not always what we need. Evolution has wired our brains to steer toward comfort and safety, so even if we're bored or burned out, we're still more likely to pay attention to those signals. But our environment also sends us signals that remind us that we're unhappy and that life could be better. We could look better, feel better, and start that business. But getting those things means making changes, and change is inherently threatening. It's safer to mutter, "Tomorrow," and then do the easy thing—sleep late, have another drink, and go back to the rotten job.

The danger zone is being just comfortable enough in your life, relationships, or career that you can convince yourself you're "good." A little comfort is okay, but being *too* comfortable is like falling into a time machine. Deep down, you know you're lying to yourself, but you're not uncomfortable enough to change things. Then you look up in horror and realize that twenty years have passed, and *nothing* has changed except your age.

I'm very aware that none of this is new. You've heard it before from motivational speakers and authors. They talk about how you have to "get outside your comfort zone" and take risks to reach your potential and have the life you want, and they're mostly right. But the idea has become such a cliché that it's tempting to roll your eyes and assume you've got this whole "get uncomfortable" thing all figured out.

You don't. Because those speakers and authors have only told you half the story. I'm going to tell you the rest.

THE REAL RISK IS REGRET

In his book *Die with Zero*, Bill Perkins writes about being in his early twenties and working at his first postcollege job at a hedge fund. One day his buddy says, "I think I'm going to take a year off and go travel in Europe." Perkins tries to talk his friend out of it, asking him what will happen to his career, and the guy responds, "I don't know. I just want to do this now." So his buddy takes off, travels to all kinds of exotic places, and has wild adventures. Two years later he comes back with all those incredible life experiences and starts over again at the bottom. Within another year he's caught up with Perkins on the corporate ladder. The buddy has lost no ground, and he's gained a lifetime's worth of peak experiences.

Perkins tells that story when he talks about minimizing regret. Regret is the other half of the story that the gurus don't tell you about. Not because they're dishonest but because they haven't thought it through. See, they convince you that your two options are:

1. Living a comfortable, safe life where you avoid risks but don't grow.
2. Choosing to be uncomfortable, risking failure, but growing and changing through experience.

If you're settling for a life you don't want because it's the path of least resistance, you're not dodging discomfort. *You're already uncomfortable.* It's just a different kind of uncomfortable. You've traded the discomfort of leaving a safe harbor, trying things you might not be good at, and putting your ass on the line for the discomfort of compromise, might-have-beens, and lifelong regret. The risk you face (and it's a big one) is getting to the end of your life and saying, "Damn, I wish I had chased my dreams." That's a tragedy. In a 1982 interview, longtime news anchor Hugh Downs said something that sums this up perfectly.

> *Don't be afraid to try something. It never hurts as bad as you think to fail. You seldom regret what you do. You regret what you didn't do. Don't try to be invulnerable. Don't worry too much about security. If you build a wall around yourself, you become a prisoner of that wall. Take a chance!*

The choice you face is not between risk and comfort. *It's between risk and regret.* There is nothing worse than regret because you can't go back and make different choices. I've worked with plenty of people who hated their careers and knew they were meant for something better but were fixated on trying to minimize the risk of leaving their job. And I get it. If you have a mortgage and a family, leaving a good-paying job is a risk you shouldn't take lightly. But while people who play defense are trying to minimize risk, people who play offense are trying to minimize regret. That's the first lesson I want to teach you in this book.

It's going to be uncomfortable either way. Yes, change will be uncomfortable, but so is complacency.

When you're making decisions, don't just consider the risk you might be taking but also the regret you could be avoiding. That's a better way to make decisions. Suppose you quit a good job to start your dream business and it fails. You can always rebuild your career. But if you stay unhappy while telling yourself you're comfortable—saying, "I'll still have that choice when I retire," or "I'll still have that chance when my kids grow up"—eventually, regret over the risks you didn't take and the life you didn't live will catch up with you. And it'll probably be when you're too old or have too many people depending on you to do anything about it.

You can have a mediocre life and never take any risks. But do you want to settle for mediocrity? If you want a great life, if you really want to see what you are capable of, make choices that increase your risk and minimize your regret. But here's an even bigger idea the self-help gurus won't even talk about:

You don't even have to be successful in your pursuit to enjoy the reward.

It's great if you can finish the marathon you trained so hard for or get to the five-year mark with your start-up. But even if you don't, you still get rewarded because *not having major regrets is the reward.*

Whoa. Mind blown, right?

It's the journey, and how the journey changes you, that matters. Think about the last time you traveled and disaster struck. When you got back home, did you talk about the easy parts of the trip? No! You bragged about how you and your friends improvised hammocks to crash at the airport and bribed a bus driver to take you to a secret beach, right?

It's the same with taking risks. Deep down, a human desire we all have is to be tested. We all feel most alive in situations where the outcome is uncertain and we have to depend on our skills, wits, and intuition. If my venture into high-performance coaching had bombed and I'd had to go back to being a fitness manager at a gym, like Bill's friend in *Die with Zero*, within a year or so, I'm confident I'd be right back where I once was. Once I confronted that reality, my worst-case scenario really wasn't all that life-altering.

There's no greater feeling than being brave enough to try what most people won't. When you look at it that way, is there even a choice?

UNCOMFORTABLE TRUTH NO. 1

Change comes with risks, but complacency comes with regret. We each have a choice.

You can accept illness, regret, and failure, or you can accept the fact that you're already uncomfortable settling for less than you know you're capable of. It's time to let go of the shame of your past failures and the fear of judgment from others and embrace the steps required to change your future.

LIFE INVENTORY

If I've shaken up your current mindset of complacency, that's a good start. But taking action is proven to be 100 percent more effective than thinking about taking action. The big issue, of course, is where to start, and I have an answer for that. The Life Inventory exercise that follows is a sort of personal GPS that will help you locate yourself on the risk-regret spectrum. My goal is to help you move past defending your decisions (and lack of decisions) so you can connect the dots and find the missing link between where you are and where you want to be. Give it a shot and allow yourself to be *brutally honest.*

1. Describe what your life looks like in the following areas:

- Career (job, income, advancement, status, passion)

____

- Body (weight, energy, health, overall conditioning, self-esteem, confidence)

- Finances (net worth, income, debt, knowledge)

- Relationships (love, partner, children, friends)

- Fulfillment (purpose, alignment, impact, experiences, life goals, doing what you enjoy)

---

2. Where would you like to be in each of these areas? (Don't hold yourself back. Be bold.)

- Career

- Body

- Finances

- Relationships

- Fulfillment

---

3. How long have you been stuck in the same place in each area?

- Career

- Body

- Finances

- Relationships

- Fulfillment

---

4. If you only had one year to live, what would you regret not pursuing or accomplishing in each of these categories?

- Career

- Body

- Finances

- Relationships

- Fulfillment

If you were honest with yourself, great work. If not, go back and stop sugarcoating it to make yourself feel better. Of course, it's hard to accept how long you've been stuck in neutral in some parts of your life, always defaulting to "This year, things will be different." The thing is, they actually can be, starting today. But not by letting days and weeks slip by.

Back in 2018 I had the privilege of seeing Robert Herjavec, one of the original sharks from *Shark Tank*, speak at George Mason University. He said some great things that day, but there was one that I've never forgotten: "There isn't that big of a difference between successful people and unsuccessful people. Successful people just don't allow themselves to have two bad days in a row."

Holy shit. That's so simple yet so mind-blowingly powerful. Successful people don't have gifts that you lack. What they do have is an intimate understanding of the thinking, emotions, and habits that can derail them and a plan for overcoming those obstacles. They're obsessed with not allowing themselves to get comfortable with having bad days. If you want to get started changing things, you don't need to have all the answers right now. Just find a win today, even if it's small.

- Send a text to a friend telling them that you're starting out to hit a specific goal in one of your categories, and ask them to check in with you in thirty days.
- Change your computer password to your savings or income goal for the year.
- Change your phone background to an image that reflects the emotion you will feel when you accomplish your goal.

I've advised hundreds of my clients to take those small steps, and not only do they love them, they work. They love that each time they key in their password, they're prompted to save, not spend. Taking small steps toward real accountability is one of the many things we're going to talk about, and here's another one: *start each day in the best way you can.* Does that mean getting up at 5:00 a.m. to work out? Maybe. But it could also mean waking up at 7:00 a.m. and journaling, eating a healthy breakfast, taking a quiet morning with your spouse instead of scrolling social media, or dozens of other things. Skyscrapers are built one bolt at a time. So are new futures.

The Life Inventory is just the beginning. I've got a lot more tough love, big ideas, and great strategies to share with you. Let's start with this fundamental question that most people have never been challenged to answer:

What does success look like for you, and how will you know when you've achieved it?

You must define that for yourself in every important category because if you don't, you will end up chasing everything and nothing at the same time.

Think about that, and think about how much longer you're willing to stay in the "uncomfort" of mediocrity, unfulfilled dreams, and regret. Because there's a more enjoyable path. It involves choosing to do things that are harder now so you'll have an easier time later, but the alternative is choosing easier now and having infinitely harder times in the future. Choose to swim out to that island. There's treasure there.

MOMENTUM BUILDERS

NOW: Change your phone background to an image, phrase, or symbol that makes you immediately think about achieving your most important goal.

TODAY: Complete the Life Inventory, show it to someone you trust, and ask them to check and confirm your brutal honesty.

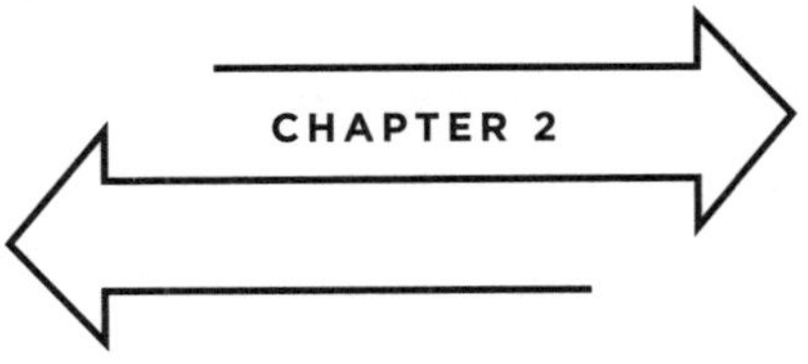

WOULD YOU RATHER . . . ?

I remember a speaking engagement back in 2018. I was speaking to a company on the topic of high-performance habits and the role they play in employee confidence and productivity. I thought I gave a decent presentation, and when I wrapped up, a handful of people thanked me for being there, for the knowledge I shared with them, and for helping to motivate them. It was solid feedback.

But when I got to my car, I sat in the parking spot in silence for about fifteen minutes (yes, this is a pattern of mine). I had an uncomfortable sense that the speech hadn't been my best. I had presented the material well and received many compliments, so why was I feeling like I had somehow cheated my audience . . . and myself? After some soul-searching, I was forced to admit that I had not shown up as 100 percent myself. I did a *good* job, but it was far from great. I knew I had held back and left some gas in the tank. I had delivered my speech as a guy I called Eighty Percent Brett.

Eighty Percent Brett did his job. He even landed a few safe jokes. But he was plain-Jane vanillaaaaa. He was unmemorable. He wasn't saying anything that a dozen other performance coaches couldn't have said. Most of all, he wasn't the me I wanted to be.

When I first started speaking, friends, family, and even some other speakers gave me advice—whether I wanted it or not. Their intent was to help me become a better speaker, but it actually led me further away from who I really was. For instance, at the time I had Tarzan-like long hair that I wore in a "man bun." A friend said, "Brett, you should cut your hair so you look more professional."

I said, "Thank you for your advice."

Another colleague said, "Dude, you need to tone down your volume and dial back some of your high energy. It might be too much for some people in the audience."

I said, "Thanks for the feedback."

Someone else said, "Lose the New Jersey accent. It's not pleasant to listen to, and people won't take you as seriously."

I said, "Fahgettaboudit!"

Not really. I said, "Thanks." But what I really wanted to say was, "Why is everyone trying to change me?" I knew they were trying to help, but I felt like now I was trying to be like so many other speakers that I was losing the parts that make me, *me*.

Baseball Hall of Famer Mickey Mantle used to tell a story about sitting next to the great Ted Williams at an All-Star Game. Mantle was a natural, instinctive athlete, while Williams was the greatest student of hitting in the history of baseball, and while they sat in the dugout during the game, Williams kept talking to Mantle about the science of hitting mechanics and all the things Mantle should try when he was at the plate. But when Mantle got back to the Yankees, he went into a two-week slump because he was trying to think about everything Williams had told him while he was at the plate.

It hit me that my friends were Ted Williams, and I was Mickey Mantle. I know, it's a bold statement to compare myself to one of the greatest baseball players of all time, but hear me out. During my presentation, I had been thinking so much about how to be more like every other speaker that it ruined my natural energy and delivery, which made me different from most speakers. That turned me into Eighty Percent Brett.

I had another speaking engagement coming up in two months, my biggest yet. The host was flying me to Florida for a weekend, and I would be the keynote speaker for a top performers event for a big financial company. At that moment, in my car, I resolved to show up as One Hundred Percent Brett for that presentation. I wouldn't hold back. I wouldn't dial down my jokes or hold back my passion and energy, even if that meant dropping a well-placed f-bomb. I would be completely, uniquely me and let the chips fall where they may. I knew it would be risky, but I had to know. Even if I bombed, at least I wouldn't regret not trying it my way.

That next presentation came and went, and I knocked it out of the park, Mickey Mantle style. The speech felt amazing and flowed so much easier than before. I was One Hundred Percent Brett. I was loud and full of energy. I walked all around the room and connected with everyone. I dropped a few well-timed curse words that caused the whole room to break out in laughter. The audience loved it because I wasn't safe, boring, or overcalculated like every other speaker they were used to. I was authentic and fun. People rushed up to me afterward and told me how refreshing it was to hear someone speak with energy and enthusiasm instead of another corporate monotone. I even booked another speaking event from someone who picked up on my Northeast slang and was also from New Jersey. That was confirmation that my intuition was right: I had brought the best version of me to the stage that day, and it was the *real* me. I decided that from that day on, I would never give any audience, client, friend, or reader any less than One Hundred Percent Brett.

CALLING BULLSHIT

We tend to think playing it safe and not offending anyone is the secret to success, especially in business. That would work if people made their decisions based on logic, but we don't. Research in areas such as relationships and the psychology of marketing show that in the end, we choose people because we like them. They're interesting. They're funny. They share our values. They're unique and have the guts and audacity we admire. That's way more important than a résumé.

Remember that the next time you decide to go into an interview, a business meeting, or a first date by hiding who you really are. Instead, go in with the best parts of your personality on full display and don't worry about being liked. Not everyone will like you or hire you, but being who you are will attract those who understand and respect you. This will also be a huge boost to your self-confidence.

WOULD YOU RATHER: GET OUT OF YOUR COMFORT ZONE OR EXPAND IT?

It was deeply uncomfortable for me to get up in front of an audience—at a speaking event that could make or break my career, no less—turn off all my filters, and just be me. But it was the kind of uncomfortable that's not only healthy but also feels really good because you're being your authentic self. We spend so much time trying to be what others expect us to be or hiding those parts of us that we think others won't approve of that we forget that the world craves authenticity. We love it when someone turns off the TikTok filters, stops trying to "sell" us, and is just a person. If it's uncomfortable to be your real self, then you need to get uncomfortable way more often! Think about how strange it is that we are attracted to the athletes, celebrities, and industry disruptors who change the game and march to the beat of their own drum, yet we spend most of our lives desperately trying to "fit in."

Pop culture talks a lot about things such as "growing in the uncomfortable" and "getting out of your comfort zone." But that oversimplifies things. So let's dig deeper. What does it mean to be uncomfortable, is there more than one way to be uncomfortable, and how can you use that feeling to get closer to your goals?

When I was a fitness trainer, I preached "getting out of your comfort zone" all the time until I realized that nothing about that phrase sounded inviting or positive. Instead, I started telling my clients we were going to "expand their comfort zone." That sounded exciting and beneficial. Most people don't want to live a life that's always uncomfortable or always challenging. But *expanding* your comfort zone means you're increasing the things in your life that you feel more comfortable doing. That's growth. If you're not comfortable speaking in front of an audience and over time you become more comfortable at it, that's one more weapon in your arsenal. That adds to your confidence and your skill set. It increases your potential.

The other thing I don't like about "getting out of your comfort zone" is that it suggests trying new things is temporary. You can step into the unknown and then step back, like you're trying on a new pair of shoes instead of a new behavior that's intended to change who you are. That's not growth; that's being a dilettante. When we think we can back away from a choice or a new behavior with no consequences, as soon as things get uncomfortable, that's exactly what we'll do. I've seen it with some of my clients.

But if we're expanding and adding to what we feel comfortable doing, that also means we're not totally turning our back on who we used to be—at least not yet. That feels less unnerving and more sustainable.

Thinking in terms of expanding their comfort zone helps many of my clients stay on course until they start to see results, which, in the case of something such as launching a business or changing careers, could take some time. Sometimes, you have to climb all the way to the top of the mountain to get the view.

WOULD YOU RATHER: EMBRACE CHANGE OR BE THE FROG IN HOT WATER?

The point is, being uncomfortable isn't as simplistic as "Do something that scares you." There are two ways of being uncomfortable, and whether you like it or not, you must choose one or the other.

My definition of discomfort is different from what most people expect. They assume the word has to do with doing things we don't like or don't want to do, such as getting out of bed at 4:00 a.m. to work out, but that's not it. Discomfort is the feeling we touched on in the previous chapter, that sense of shame and disappointment that comes with knowing you could be better, fitter, happier, richer, or whatever "er," but you can't get out of your own way. You're leaving life on the table, and you know it, and it eats at you daily. That's *discomfort.*

If you don't think that sounds too bad, think about the old parable about the frog in the hot water. If you heat the water to boiling and then drop in the frog, the frog will freak out and jump out of the pot, right? That's what we do when we face immediate, radical change. But if you put the frog into the water when it's lukewarm and then raise the temperature a little at a time, the frog gets used to the rising temperatures, so it just sits there until it cooks and dies. That's what we do when we accept that "you are where you are" and the general suckiness of life—we rationalize, we stop trying, we freeze in place, and, eventually, we become numb and lose our ability to change anything.

Discomfort is living with the knowledge that you've given up *trying* to improve those areas of your life where you *know* you can do better. Trying is succeeding because just making the effort improves mood and self-esteem, breaks us out of unproductive routines, starts us on the road to developing new disciplines, gives us a new perspective, and usually produces some positive results. A woman who gets sidetracked three months into a six-month fitness plan still improves her conditioning, builds some muscle, and loses some weight. A guy who only gets halfway to a big financial goal has still saved some money or paid down some debt. Life isn't an all-or-nothing game. We measure progress by our willingness to embrace change, so the only failure is in not trying at all.

UNCOMFORTABLE TRUTH NO. 2

Life is passing you by as you continue to wait for the perfect time to begin.

New Year's resolutions are a waste of time—not because of the resolutions part but because you buy into the hype that January is special. You make a promise to yourself that you know you're not going to keep, then repeat the same mistakes as the last time, thinking those four awful words: "This time it's different." But it's not. Thinking your willpower will somehow be stronger is self-delusion. If you want to get different results, change your environment and put accountability systems in place on a random Tuesday. Then if that doesn't work, have a plan B and a plan C. Forget about January 1. People who only start new things on a Monday or at the beginning of a year or month are often the ones who struggle with this the most. Drop the idea that there is ever a perfect time to start and start yesterday.

WOULD YOU RATHER: RUN THROUGH THE MUD OR SIT IN IT?

The best way to describe uncomfort is to go back to what I was feeling after that speech where I showed up as Eighty Percent Brett. Sitting in my car that day and realizing I could have been better, given more, and impacted my audience in an even greater way was more uncomfortable than the idea of walking to the podium at 100 percent, knowing that not everyone would embrace that version of me. That was a scary prospect but not as scary as the prospect of always wondering, "What if . . . ?"

Uncomfort is the uneasy excitement we feel when we decide to hold nothing back, not knowing what will happen and trusting that going for it is the right thing to do. We know we're going to have a few white-knuckle moments, but we choose to lean into them. We override our desire to run away because we trust—either from experience or from the wisdom we've absorbed from those who have gone before us—that being uncomfortable about change is to be expected and that on the other side of that feeling lies massive growth and positive change.

Here's how I define uncomfort:

> *An exhilarating uneasiness that comes from choosing to put yourself in situations where you're forced to adapt, fail, make mistakes, and learn but where you're actually in control and there are rewards at the end, such as pride, self-esteem, experience, and achievement.*

We're all conflicted. We want the result, but we don't want to have to change to get the result. Making the choice and following it up with actions sounds simple, but remember that we're naturally disposed to comfort. The result is this continual game of mental ping-pong, back and forth, from choice to self-sabotage to regret to choosing all over again.

How do you end that cycle? By making a choice, once and for all, between discomfort and uncomfort. It's a simple choice but not an easy one. When we avoid conflict, challenges, confronting our failures, and getting out of our zone of predictability, we think we're avoiding discomfort, but we're not. We're neck-deep in it. Instead of running through a mud puddle, we end up sitting in it. We freeze in place and become fossilized, aware that we're failing ourselves but feeling more and more powerless to get moving again as time goes by. Who would choose that?

But plenty of people choose to seek out uncomfort. In recent years, psychologists have taken to studying improv theater to see how deliberately experiencing uncomfortable situations affects personal growth. It turns out that in a study of more than two thousand people, most of those who took improv classes reported emotional growth, increased self-confidence, a greater willingness to confront difficult emotions, more openness to opposing political viewpoints, and other signs of personal development. The key was, these folks *chose* to be uncomfortable. They took action. They went out of their way to challenge themselves instead of sitting on the couch, making lists, and ultimately doing nothing.

Remember the children's book series and TV show *The Magic School Bus*? I'd watch episodes when I was home sick from school as a kid. The epic mantra of the forever encouraging teacher, Ms. Frizzle, was "Take chances! Make mistakes! Get messy!" That's uncomfort in a nutshell.

THE THREE LEVELS OF FRUSTRATION

As you try to navigate the journey from discomfort to uncomfort, it's helpful to have markers that remind you of where you are. One of them is *frustration*. There are three levels, and the one you're in right now can tell you a lot about what you need to do next.

Level 1: You're not frustrated. Whatever is happening isn't bothering you. But maybe you're in denial or too busy to notice your suffering. Time to take a minute, step back, and honestly assess if you're really happy and satisfied with your current situation or just refusing to look at reality.

Level 2: You're frustrated enough to complain but not uncomfortable enough to make major changes. You might be stuck in complacency or a vicious cycle of bad habits, but you're stuck. This is when to start thinking about the price of uncomfort versus the cost of staying stuck.

Level 3: You're frustrated to the point of being willing to change things and make sacrifices. Maybe you're pissed, tired, or fed-up. This is when you want to channel that frustration, face the hard truths, and make a plan. When you see that you're this frustrated, look closer. What have you been complaining about? That might be the uncomfort that you need to embrace.

WOULD YOU RATHER: TREAD WATER INDEFINITELY OR SWIM TO SHORE?

I have bad news and good news. The bad news is, you have to choose. No matter what you do, you're going to be uncomfortable in your life. The question is: Which way of being uncomfortable will you choose? You can choose uncomfort, where you take a long look in the mirror, set tough goals, do what's hard, adapt on the fly, and grow through challenge and adversity. Or you can choose discomfort, where you're living your worst-case scenario every day, knowing you could be more and have all the power to change your situation but never having the guts to try.

It's a real-life game of *would you rather* that you cannot avoid. It takes just as much energy to sit and complain about something every day and do nothing about it as it does to make a decision and start trying to improve your situation. It's the difference between treading water and swimming to shore. They both require energy and effort; only one is keeping you stationary and stuck exactly where you are, while the other is moving you toward a solution and an improved situation.

The good news? Choosing uncomfort doesn't mean being uncomfortable all the time. Nobody can do that. I love routine as much as anyone, and there is nothing wrong with relaxing at the end of a long day. But you will enjoy it more when it's the reward for the full day you've had and the disciplined plan you followed. Choosing uncomfort means being open to new habits and new experiences that push your abilities and lead you into areas where you're not proficient—yet. In improv comedy, it means saying, "Yes" when you're tempted to say, "Uh, I'll just stay over here in the corner."

One great example of this is a gentleman named Wesley Hamilton. You might remember him as the smiling, wheelchair-bound bodybuilder from season three of *Queer Eye*. He was already an impressive guy in the show, but he's even more impressive when you know his backstory. Before he lost his ability to walk, Wes admitted he was a gun-toting thug on the streets of Kansas City. Then at twenty-four, a misunderstanding over a girl led to him getting shot, leaving him permanently paralyzed from the waist down.

At that point Wes could have chosen the discomfort of surrendering to his terrible new circumstances, maybe as his punishment for being a bad guy. He could have spent the rest of his life in a hospital bed. But he didn't. He chose uncomfort. He lost one hundred pounds just by changing his diet. He started working out, got jacked, became a disabled CrossFit champ and a fitness model, and started a nonprofit called Disabled But Not Really that advocates for gym accessibility and fitness training for people with disabilities. Wes will even tell you that he's *grateful* for being shot because it changed the course of his life.

Choosing uncomfort gives you power; choosing discomfort takes your power away. You become complacent, and complacency is the killer of potential greatness. You go along for years, telling yourself that one of these days, you'll get your act together and change things. But that day never comes. Then all of a sudden, the consequences of inaction land with a thud: burnout, bankruptcy, divorce, or a heart attack.

You've got to choose. If not for yourself, then do it for the people around you, the people you have the power to influence. For example, what are you telling your kids by not going after something that's going to make you happier? Are you telling them that it's better to stay in a safe job you hate because you've been there for ten years—that it's more important than doing something that's going to make you significantly happier? Wouldn't you rather your kids or partner see you wake up every day happy and excited, doing something you're passionate about and great at? Think about this:

You never know who you're inspiring simply by the way you choose to live your life.

If you read chapters 1 and 2 of this book and never read anything else, but you choose to lean into more uncomfort in life, your life will improve. I guarantee it. Remember, harder now equals easier later.

MOMENTUM BUILDERS

NOW: Now is the perfect time to choose one area from your Life Inventory exercise in chapter 1 (career, body, finances, relationships, fulfillment) where you are going to lean into uncomfort. Where have you been treading water, stuck at level 2 frustration, and continuing to complain but not take action? Write down exactly what this issue or situation is and identify why you've been complaining about it.

TODAY: Identify one small action you can begin to take to start swimming to shore. This action needs to take you three minutes or less to complete. Think baby steps: logging into your checking account and looking at the numbers, writing down your dream job, finding your workout sneakers, or writing down your goal. For many of you, this action might be your first small taste of uncomfort. Congratulations, you're already making progress.

YOU HAVEN'T TRIED EVERYTHING; YOU'VE JUST TRIED EVERYTHING YOU CAN THINK OF

I wrote this chapter because, despite all the obvious reasons to do it, it's really hard to convince people to choose uncomfort. So I'm going to paint a helpful picture of what happens when you make that choice. But to me, it's really not even a choice. If you decide to stay in discomfort—and are admittedly okay with stagnation, inevitable decline, denial, regret, and unrealized potential—why are you even reading this book? Hopefully you are open-minded about the power of making positive changes in your life and becoming an even better version of yourself.

Since you've read this far, let's assume that discomfort is off the table and you're ready to lean into uncomfort.

When you first choose uncomfort, one of the first things that happens is a series of reality checks that will probably make you want to flip me the bird and change your mind. Because you don't get to hide behind comforting self-delusions and empty promises anymore. You don't get to tell yourself, "Next month, I'll work out five days a week" or "I'll quit my job at the end of June and start my company" and have nobody hold you accountable. Now you've actually got to make a plan and put it into action. Sometimes, that's a startling, difficult mental shift.

Back when I was working as a fitness trainer, one of my most difficult but rewarding clients was a forty-year-old single dad who was strong-willed and stubborn as all hell but claimed he wanted to make big changes. While I was putting him through his workouts, I would also use our time to sharpen my life-coaching skills and try to chip away at the other twenty-three hours of his day. He talked a lot about his drinking and partying. At this point, I had cut out a lot of the alcohol in my own life and even gone two years without drinking at all. But this client always told me, "I'll do everything else, but I won't give up drinking. I'll do sit-ups and change my diet, but I'll never give up drinking." But eventually, after months of getting peppered with questions about it, he agreed to pause his drinking just to see what it would be like.

Once he did, he was like, "Holy crap, Brett, you weren't lying. Staying in shape is not nearly as hard as I've been making it all these years." Once he cut out most of the booze, he started drinking a lot more water and staying hydrated, which meant he got better results from his workouts and got injured less often. He started sleeping better. Then he started to realize that when he wasn't drinking, he had less in common with the circle of friends with whom he drank. He found himself gravitating toward people who were doing morning workouts and living healthy. He also had a young son, and he told me that after he gave up drinking, he was spending more quality time with his son, as opposed to being in the room but being on his phone or, even worse, being hungover. His son would even jump in at the end of our sessions, which I thought was really cool.

All sorts of good things started to happen for this guy, and finally, he said, "Brett, I really thought you were full of shit, but there might really be something to this drinking less thing." Over the next six months, he continued making small change after small change. Eventually, his family finally saw so many positive changes in him that they asked to drop in on one of our workouts to thank me personally. He's come so far, and while I don't work with him anymore, we still stay in touch. I've spoken at his company on multiple occasions. To say I'm proud of him is an understatement. He was also proof to me that even someone dead set in their ways can change, as soon as they are willing to embrace getting uncomfortable and admit they haven't tried everything.

PROGRESS HIDES IN SPACES WHERE YOU RESIST GOING

My client thought he had tried everything to feel better and be a better father, but in reality, he really hadn't tried very much. Everybody loves to say, "I've tried everything," but it's just not true. In fact, that thing you haven't had the nerve to try yet is where you will always find your best return on investment (ROI). That's why choosing uncomfort is so difficult. Giving up things you don't care about is easy. But anything you get is worth the price you pay for it, so why would you expect major life changes to come from giving up or changing things that don't matter to you?

My client didn't want to stop drinking. For the longest time, it was a hard line in the sand for him. When he finally did, it changed everything. Is there something you've been resisting changing because you haven't been willing to go there? It could be quitting drinking or watching TV, changing your circle of friends, or giving up social media. It could be showing up for your job with better energy or finally quitting and finding a better one.

Refusing to go to those forbidden places leads people to assume there's only one way to have a fulfilling career, get in great shape, or have a happy marriage. That's not true. There are as many different strategies as there are people *if* you're willing to try the things you've been too afraid or stubborn to try in the past. If you've gone down the same road again and again and not gotten the results you want, try something different.

Some people end up testing out six, seven, or ten different methods for sticking to a weight loss plan or paying off debt before they find something that works.

That's what I mean when I say that your real ROI will probably come when you try an approach that you haven't tried before, or with a level of consistency you've never shown before. *Progress hides in the spaces where you resist going.* Why do you resist? Maybe you have a habit that's tough to quit, such as cigarettes. Maybe you want to avoid bringing up bad memories or dodge guilt over past failures. Maybe you don't want the pushback from friends or family. But building a wall around certain habits or behaviors is usually about *identity.*

You've become the fun person who drinks with friends every weekend or who works eighty hours a week to cover up your failing marriage. You can't stop doing that thing because it's too big a part of who you are. Complaining about your weight or your job is part of it too. Clients have even admitted to me that without their weight to complain about, they didn't know what their lives would look like, or what they would use as an excuse in other areas of their life they were unhappy with! That part of their identity had become a crutch, and believe it or not, complaining about it was how they got attention.

Whatever the reason, when you take some options off the table, you're flying a big flag that says, "This is where all the growth-preventing fears, false beliefs, or insecurities are!" Visiting that dimly lit mental storeroom isn't easy. I know that. That's why it's so important to have someone in your life who holds you accountable and convinces you to go there, flip the light on, and confront all that stuff you've been avoiding. Because there, in the uncomfort, is where you find challenge, self-discovery, learning, perspective, growth, new habits, discipline, and confidence, tucked away in the attic of your mind, just waiting to be discovered.

CALLING BULLSHIT

Everybody talks about *self-control* as the critical ingredient in making change stick. *Wrong.* Okay, then it must be *progress*, right? *Nope*, not quite. But there is one element that is common to almost everyone who finds their way to long-lasting change in their life, health, career, and relationships. It's curiosity. People who embrace uncomfort are almost always open-minded and curious about what change would look like for them. Their curiosity at what the future could bring outweighs their anxiety over changing their spending habits or quitting their job. They're always saying, "What would it be like for me if I did that?"

HAVE YOU TRIED EMBRACING A NEW IDENTITY?

I know from experience how hard it can be to let go of a part of your identity. All my life I had been a multi-sport athlete. That changed when I got hurt. I had always been the kid who got recognition for scoring points and for being the man on the court or the field or the diamond, and now all of a sudden, who the hell was I? Who was going to say, "Good game, Brett" or "Great hustle out there, number five"? I overcorrected for this sudden loss of identity by becoming an angry troublemaker, acting out, and spending time in the wrong places, but my coaches and my mom thankfully pulled me back from that.

My coaches were amazing. They challenged me about the kind of teammate I had been since I got my diagnosis. They said, "You're still an athlete. You're still required to be at practice. We need you to be part of this team." That opened my eyes. Once I saw that I could change my identity over and over and become a new version of myself while still being me, the pressure of making big decisions diminished, and the awesome life I have today became possible.

That experience showed me that the happiest people in the world are the ones who know who they are and are open to changing and embracing new identities throughout life. If you cling to one identity forever, life leaves you behind. I try to teach my clients a new vocabulary to describe themselves. If they say, "I'm divorced," I'll gently correct them and say, "No, you've gone through a divorce. It's not a scarlet letter that you have to wear." If they say, "I'm overweight," and I help them change their language to "I'm on a journey to weight loss and improved fitness," that feels less like a verdict and more like a possibility.

Uncomfort leads to positive change and to the process we'll follow for the rest of the book. Here's what that looks like:

Acknowledging your barriers. The first step is always looking in the mirror, looking at your past, and accepting your role in creating the barriers that have gotten in the way of your goals. That's how you create new systems and solutions that kick down those barriers. Until you are able to do this, you will continue to be your own worst enemy by blaming everyone but yourself and prevent any real changes from occurring.

Setting goals the right way. Some goals intimidate us into inaction. Saying, "I'm going to pay off my $20,000 credit card debt this year," might as well be, "I'm going to climb Mount Everest barefoot this year." Some goals require a process because you can't just snap your fingers and make them happen. What you can do is say, "I'm going to track my credit-card spending and pay $500 a month until everything is paid off." We'll work on setting goals that are aspirational yet specific and achievable.

Planning for failure. You know the old saying, "People don't plan to fail; they fail to plan"? Well, around here we do both. When you choose uncomfort and start trying methods to reach your goals that you've been reluctant to try, you're going to fail. You're going to cheat, backslide, and be tempted to give up. When those things happen (and they will), what's your plan to keep going? We'll make one.

Setting up consequences and accountability. Many people fail to reach goals because they underestimate how hard it will be. Remember, your body and mind long for the status quo; they don't want to change. It's important to put accountability systems in place so there are consequences for cheating or breaking a promise to yourself. But it's just as important to set up rewards for when you do well or hit a milestone.

Taking the first step into action, reaching milestones, and continuing progress. Setting strict timelines when seeking goals can often backfire. Why? Because progress is almost never in a straight line. We do well for a while, then slip, pause, get hurt. Life happens. That's why just putting your plan in motion—and keeping it in motion—is more important than reaching an arbitrary goal in a set amount of time. If you and your partner go to therapy consistently for a year, you *will* have a stronger relationship. If you work out and eat right consistently for a year, you *will* have better results next time you have a physical. Sticking with the process (and enjoying the changes) is the most important goal.

These are the building blocks, the timbers that hold up the building. But like any building, there's a lot more work that has to be done before we can call it complete.

UNCOMFORTABLE TRUTH NO. 3

You've gotten way too comfortable losing.

Losing the morning. Losing your workout. Losing your day. Losing is contagious. Let that sink in and start to sting. When you lose, you need to get back on the winning side—now. How? Make the game smaller. Instead of trying to do it all in one day, pick one area where you know you can get a win under your belt. Start racking up some small wins and remind yourself of how freakin' good it feels to win. That's *also*

> contagious. Aim small, miss small. The most dangerous thing you can do is get numb to losing. Losing should feel shitty. It should make you furious that you broke a commitment to yourself. That's the only way you avoid getting comfortable with losing.

HAVE YOU TRIED LEANING IN?

For two years in my early thirties, after I had started working for myself, I became a part-time boxing instructor. What seemed like a step back to others provided me with two things. One, it gave me the opportunity to be part of a team again, and two, I was able to log hundreds of reps motivating people using the headset microphone and small stage. Being a group fitness instructor taught me so much about throwing yourself into new experiences and learning as you go.

At the time I knew nothing about boxing or how to box other than a few scrappy bar fights I had to break up when I worked as a bouncer in college. When I was struggling to learn the proper footwork and land my punches during sparring, Julian, my boxing coach, told me, "Brett, you'll never land punches or have any opportunity to defeat your opponent unless you have the courage to *lean in*." Julian was my real-life Mr. Miyagi, and I was lost somewhere between wax on and wax off. He went on to explain that leaning in, while giving me the best chance to land my own punches, also made me more vulnerable to getting punched myself. The most successful boxers understood that to win, it was necessary to face the fear head-on and have the courage to take some punches.

At the time I had zero intention of getting in the ring; however, I quickly realized the larger and even more impactful benefit of this *lean in* analogy. Throughout life you will face many different and challenging *opponents* against whom you could easily lean back, remain comfortably protected on the sidelines of life, and remove yourself from any real chance to compete, win, or succeed. Or you could go toe-to-toe with the uncomfortable, face it head-on and lean in, take some punches along the way, and give yourself a fighting chance to create the life you know you want.

Leaning in will be a helpful mantra to keep in your back pocket. The other big building block is knowing the stages you're likely to go through on this journey from discomfort to uncomfort. Right off the bat, it's important to understand that before you can change something, you have to accept that change is possible, acceptable, and beneficial. You'll go through times when you don't want to do this and you're tempted to go back to your old life, so it's crucial to establish a mantra, such as "I'm going to be better off when I give up whatever I've been clinging to and fully lean into this process of embracing new things." Because you will be.

Now let's talk about the stages you're likely to experience. First, there's ***refusal to part with your current identity.*** The longer you've been doing something, the more comforting it is, even if it's bad for you. You're going to want to hold on to habits or people that don't serve you and make bargains with yourself in order to keep them, such as "I'll only eat fast food on weekends." That's a slippery slope, but it will be easier to manage if you replace old habits with new ones.

Next is ***curiosity about what change might look like.*** You're not convinced that uncomfort is for you, but now you're wondering what it would feel like to be out of debt, have a job you love, or be in better shape. That's good.

The third stage is ***seeing what's possible.*** Once you get your head out of a denial space and start looking around, you can see success stories—people you know who've started businesses, completely transformed their bodies, and made major life upgrades.

That leads to the next stage: ***I'm going to give this a shot.*** Now you're ready to make a plan, remake your environment, commit, and get going on a program of change.

This is where things get interesting. The next stage is the fun one: ***the honeymoon phase.*** You're all fired up because you're starting out on a journey into the new and unknown, and the hard work—and the reality of giving stuff up—hasn't hit yet. You feel positive and empowered, convinced that you've already made progress by saying yes. And you have . . . sort of.

But now you reach the stage where ***your old habits, peers, and environment start to push back.*** This is a big one. The psychological and physiological conditioning from your old life is still hanging around. You crave the junk you used to eat. You're dying to text your ex. You want the dopamine hit of buying something expensive and having packages arrive at your door. Environmental changes can help by removing temptation, but you also need a "worst day" action plan: call the person who holds you accountable, look at old pictures of yourself, check your bank account—anything to get you over those temporary hurdles.

You'll also get pressure from the people in your life. Some of your friends will resent the changes you're making and even accuse you of judging them. When my client quit drinking, his friends were like, "Dude, what are you doing? Why aren't you drinking, and why are you leaving so early?" He would go to a party, and even though his buddies knew what he was doing, they would offer him a drink when he got there, offer again halfway through, and offer one more time at the end of the night. This continued for months because they were convinced he would eventually cave and probably wanted him to.

When I first got really into fitness and healthy eating, I experienced the same thing. I would go out with my guy friends to watch football, and everybody would order wings, mozzarella sticks, and pizza, and I would order a cobb salad. I wasn't trying to make anybody feel bad, but my boys still gave me a hard time. However, here's the irony: the same people who are dogging you the hardest will be the ones texting you a year from now asking for advice on how you got your results.

If you can get past those last two stages, you'll get to the next, ***early results***. You're not at the finish line yet, but you can see progress. Your credit card balance is lower. You have a job interview you're excited about. Your jeans fit better. Early results are never as dramatic as your expectations make them, so it's important to make sure those expectations are realistic. But they give you hope and keep you going.

That's vital because of the next stage: *Whoops!* You get so excited about making early progress that you decide to reward yourself, and for a day, you go back to old habits. You grab a glass of wine, skip a workout, buy just that one thing, whatever. Then you beat yourself up, and if you're not careful, it's enough to make you quit. This is when it's important to remember that success doesn't happen in a straight line. Setbacks and speed bumps are to be expected. The key is to not be seduced by perfectionism, see that one mistake isn't the end of the world, and get back on your plan the next day—or, better yet, immediately.

If you can get through all these stages and reach the ninety-day mark, you should see what I call ***affirming results***. These are identity-altering results that prove to you that this was all worth it. You're seeing a fitter body and a growing bank account. You've also developed new, positive habits and a new routine. But something even more powerful has happened . . . you've changed your identity. You're now a person who can vow to change things and actually follow through!

Enough stage setting. Turn the page, choose uncomfort, and let's get busy.

MOMENTUM BUILDERS

NOW: What part of your identity have you been clinging to that is no longer serving you? Why is the thought of giving up this piece of you making you so uneasy? Or perhaps there is a new identity you've been wanting to step into but have been avoiding fully embracing. Write down that new identity.

TODAY: What's one area or change you've tried to make where you can now admit that you haven't tried everything? Identify that one line in the sand you've been refusing to cross, and challenge yourself to remain open-minded and curious about the positive outcomes that could exist on the other side of that line.

PART II

GOOD NEWS—YOU'RE THE PROBLEM

YOUR ENVIRONMENT IS YOUR ENEMY

Before I missed basically an entire calendar year of high school sports because of injury, I had been dead set on getting an athletic scholarship to a division one university. By the time I was a senior, it was obvious that wasn't going to happen, so I started looking at division three schools where I could potentially play football or basketball. There was a school just under two hours away from my home: Rowan University in Glassboro, New Jersey. My two best friends were going there. Plus, my sister was already off at college, so it was just my mom and me. After the injury and losing my dad, I had made up my mind that I would stay close to home so I could visit often since my mom would now be all alone in our house.

Because of that, I didn't take the college application process very seriously. I didn't think about the impact of those four years. It was just the next small decision I had to make. But my older cousin had transferred into James Madison University in Harrisonburg, Virginia. He was a couple of years older than me, and I always looked up to him. He said,

"Dude, you have to apply here. You would absolutely love it here." But the school was over a five-hour drive away, and that was not in the cards for me anymore. Still, I applied to make him happy (and so he would stop asking me) and reluctantly agreed to visit him and the campus.

JMU blew my mind. It was everything I thought a college would look and feel like. I fell in love with it. I spent the night there with my cousin, and the beautiful campus and social scene were like something out of a movie. But every time my mom would ask about college, I would say, "Rowan's fine. I'll play football or basketball." I didn't want to worry her with the idea that I might move far away, and I wasn't going to allow myself to get my hopes up, so I pushed the whole decision off. Then I surprisingly got accepted to JMU, and my mom and my sister convinced me to go back for a second visit. There were a lot of exciting things going on at the school; even my mom felt the vibe. She was starting to see that the school had a lot to offer me.

On the drive home, my mom was weirdly hyping and pushing JMU now, saying things such as "You seem like you really like it here." Meanwhile, I was trying not to admit it, to her or myself, saying stuff such as "Whatever, it was fine. They have some of the cool majors you like there. That was fun." I had also found out how expensive JMU was, especially since I wouldn't be playing sports or eligible for in-state New Jersey tuition like I would be at Rowan.

Finally, my mom said, "Well, I sure hope you like it as much as I think you do." I snapped back, "Mom, why does it matter what I like? I'm going to Rowan."

She said, "No. Actually, you're going to JMU because I already paid your freshman year tuition."

"WHAT!" I freaked out. I couldn't believe she had done that without asking me. I was so mad that I was actually arguing with her about it! But at the same time, I was excited. She was right—that *was* where I wanted to go. I knew I belonged there. But she knew I'd never admit that to her. It meant moving five hours away, and with my sister going into her senior year, also meant my mom would be completely alone in the house for the first time. The older I get, the more I appreciate how selfless a decision that was, especially given our situation. Even for a mom. Even now, writing this, my eyes still well up with tears when I think of her doing that for me. She had to know how impactful that decision would be on the rest of my life.

CALLING BULLSHIT

You've heard the whole "It takes 10,000 hours to master something" trope, right? Well, nobody ever focuses on where the biggest learning curve of that 10,000 hours happens. It happens in the first 20 hours. The other 9,980 hours are just practice and repetition. You might not reach 10,000 hours in many areas, but that doesn't mean you can't learn enough to be proficient. I always encourage people to get that first 20 hours out of the way as quickly as possible. Don't be gradual. Don't spread your first 20 hours of working out or learning a new skill over a year. Burn through them in the first month or as fast as you can, while you're still exhilarated and open to anything. By the end of those 20 hours, you'll be so much more confident in any area you apply this to. You'll have so much more courage. You'll have so much more knowledge.

TENSION IS YOUR ALLY

I don't think I have to explain to you the gift my mom gave me that day. I was always the kid who wanted to explore and travel and who dreamed of big adventures. To quote my favorite movie, *A Knight's Tale*, I dreamed of "changing my stars." But I think that if my mother had let me go to Rowan, I would've gone to school with my best friends from high school. I would've been a big fish in a small pond, just like in high school. I would've played sports, had a lot of friends, and walked away in four years with a degree. There was a chance I would have been basically the same person I was when I went in as a freshman.

But because my mom saw an opportunity and pushed me out of where I was comfortable, I had a completely different experience. I had to adapt to living in a new state and a different campus culture. I expanded my mind. I was able to establish a new identity; I wasn't the kid who got hurt and lost his dad anymore. I was like everybody else. That gave me an opportunity to test myself and spread my wings. It was her way of telling me, "Brett, I'm going to be okay. You need to go live your life."

Right now, there is tension between who you are today and who you believe you have the potential to become. While it's great to believe you can be healthier, wealthier, and happier, in the end your belief doesn't change much if you don't act on it. You can make lists and repeat affirmations into the mirror all you want, and that won't have as much of an impact on your future as finding a way to start your business or set foot in the gym.

Here's the thing: Tension is a source of energy. Tension either continues or resolves. The best example of this is in music. When you hear a series of chords in a song, and they don't resolve (by returning to the same key the song began in, for instance), you feel tension. Things feel unfinished, incomplete. If the tension goes on, the music is infused with potential energy, even becoming a little uncomfortable. Then when the chord progression finally resolves to C major, there's a sense of relief. You sigh and relax because it feels right.

When you choose uncomfort and try to change the trajectory of your life, you're going to face constant pressure to go back to the way you were. It's inevitable. So it's critical that you not relax, settle, or become static and satisfied with the way things are. You have to stay in a state of tension by constantly challenging yourself. How? *By changing your current environment.*

Here's a mindblower for you:

Your current environment is perfectly calibrated to keep you exactly the same person you are today by making you think you're comfortable.

Whoa, right? It's true. When it comes to change, resistance is your biggest competitor. The outcome of your battle with resistance often hinges on your environment. Most people greatly underestimate the difficulty of changing themselves while remaining in an old environment. It's like attempting to overcome a gambling addiction while sitting inside the casino, staring at the poker chips. The easier path? Change your environment first and let it support and reinforce the new habits and behaviors you're seeking.

I learned that when my mom gave me the motherly gift of kicking me out of New Jersey and sending me to JMU. I wasn't in my comfortable, familiar environment anymore, and that forced me to learn and grow twice as fast. Four years later, I came back home for two quick years and then jumped at the opportunity to make another move, this time to the Washington, DC, area, where two of my former roommates were heading to accept jobs. I didn't have a job lined up, but I knew that when I went back to my hometown, it felt like everyone was doing the same thing every night. The same people were always at the same bar.

Don't get me wrong, I'm incredibly proud to be from my hometown and love New Jersey. However, I started to feel like if I wasn't the first one to leave, I would end up being the last one left. I would see people in the bar who were five years older than me, complacent, comfortable, overweight, sharing the same old stories and talking about their big plans but not *doing* anything about them. I didn't want that to be me.

I knew I ultimately wanted to move somewhere warm, live by the beach, and chase my biggest dreams, but I also knew that right then, moving to DC was the easiest, fastest way for me to get out of my hometown and get uncomfortable again. My mom said, "Go spread your wings. I'm fine. Be smart and *don't forget who you are.*" She would say that to me every time I left the house. While she never explained to me what she meant by it, I believe that was her simple reminder for me to make decisions with integrity, not allow my gifts and experiences to go to waste, and remember that I'm stronger than I even realize. So I moved back to Virginia. But if I hadn't gone to JMU first, I never would've met the guys who invited me to move, and I never would've eventually relocated to San Diego and then to Florida to live my ocean-air beach dream.

UNCOMFORTABLE TRUTH NO. 4

We only see what we want to see.

If all those limiting factors, such as the food in your fridge or those credit card offers that tempt you to overspend, have always been there, why haven't you seen them until now? *Because you didn't look.* We see what we're looking for, and few people willingly look at things that make them feel guilt or regret. The fact is, if you had looked at the numbers on the bathroom scale or your bank balance as much as you look at Instagram or TikTok, you'd have figured out a long time ago that things were in need of a change.

FRICTION IS YOUR FRIEND

The way you stay in that state of tension, always adapting and challenging yourself, is by changing everything about your environment that's keeping you the way you don't want to be. You're not only discarding the things that are holding you back, but you're also cleaning out the temptations and introducing new things and people that make you feel more focused, confident, and inspired.

Do you have to do this? *Yes*. What you want for yourself comes at a cost. Wants by themselves are like a Christmas list—you're waiting for Santa to bring you something without having to do anything for it. But there's a reason adults stop sending their lists to Santa.

Wanting is free. Earning something comes at a price.

When you say, "I want this, and here's what I'm willing to do to get it," you create a completely different mentality. Now you're thinking the right way: *What price am I willing to pay to be who I want to be and have what makes me happy?*

Part of that price is making radical, permanent changes to your environment. Some examples of what I mean are as follows:

- The food in your kitchen
- Your living environment
- Your sleeping environment
- Your morning routine
- What you watch and listen to
- Your relationship with your cell phone
- The people you spend the most time with

Suppose you're ready to embark on a journey of uncomfort and big change, and you choose to focus on a big goal that's eluded you for years: training for and running a marathon, for example. To increase your chances of success, you decide to do a Marie Kondo–style makeover of big parts of your life that have been holding you back. You know you need lots of healthy carbohydrates and lean protein to fuel your training runs and build muscle, so you box up all the garbage in your fridge and donate it to a food pantry. You replace it with lots of brown rice, sweet potatoes, a variety of fruits, and proteins such as chicken and fish. You also know you'll need to drink massive amounts of water, so you buy a new sexy half-gallon water bottle in bright orange that will never leave your side, ensuring that you'll drink a gallon of water per day.

Sleep will be important for your recovery, so you change your bedroom. You move your TV and computer to another room, install blackout curtains, and download a smartphone app that tracks your sleep cycles and makes suggestions for you to get more restorative sleep. You buy an actual alarm clock to avoid using your phone in bed and set it for 5:00 a.m., your wake-up time for a 5:30 a.m. run. You go to a running store and get custom running shoes fitted to your feet, an important step to prevent injury. You start keeping your running gear and shoes right beside your bed so they're the first things you see when you wake up. Finally, you join a running club and start hanging around other people training for long-distance races.

None of these steps guarantee that you'll be ready for a marathon or that you'll finish. What they do is *reduce friction*, clearing out every potential obstacle that stands between where you are today and your future goal. Changing your environment not only keeps you in a state of productive tension, but it also eliminates as much friction as possible: temptations, inconveniences, distractions, things that undercut your confidence. By getting rid of things that create friction, you're increasing the odds that you'll build momentum and sustain it.

BUILD A BRIDGE, NOT A WALL

But it's not only things and routines you need to clear out of your environment. The hard part of this process is the boundaries you will need to create with the people who keep you down, create doubt, pull you back toward old habits, and hurt your self-confidence. Your job is to replace them with people who lift you up, challenge you, understand your goals, and restore your energy.

I think of the people you currently spend most of your time with as "the people on your bus." The image of you driving your bus through life is a reminder that the direction and speed of your bus must be up to you, and the people on that bus at any given time will make it easier or harder to reach your desired destination. Who's riding on your bus, and what impact is each of them having on you? Take an "energy inventory" of the people you hang out with and work with. Are you spending time with people who encourage you, set positive examples for you, and hold you accountable? Or are you wasting time with people who take energy from you with negative talk, who tempt you to cheat on your nutrition plan or sobriety plan, or who actually try to sabotage you because you're doing something they haven't had the guts to do? Ask Siri or ChatGPT to explain the phrase "crabs in a bucket," and you'll understand this perfectly.

There's an old saying, "You are who you hang with." It's true. If you go all in on uncomfort and stick to your plan for change and success, you won't want to spend as much time around the kind of people I used to see in my hometown bar. You might catch a game with them once in a while, but don't be surprised if you begin to realize that you don't want to commit the weeks and hours to the fantasy football league anymore. You may start to get tired of participating in complaint-filled conversations about politics and the government. You'll naturally begin to crave the company of other doers, people who want more from life and share your same goals and determination, people who are driving in the same direction as you.

Does that sound a little cold, maybe a little ruthless? *It is.* But this is serious business. This is real talk about your life, that thing you only get one of. This is a matter of survival, of building the kind of life that brings you joy and success. You can't do that in your old environment surrounded by people who don't have the same life vision as you.

Clearing the negative, sabotaging, and time-wasting people off your bus and out of your life forces you to confront issues you'd rather avoid, such as past poor decisions, impostor syndrome, and alleged "friends" who find it easier to be part of the demolition squad than the builders. You know, the folks in the cheap seats who lack the courage to step into the arena and build their own dreams, so they'd rather demolish yours, pass judgment, and make you feel bad for pursuing your ambitions. You'll find these keyboard heroes on any social media platform as well.

How do you get those people off your bus? You keep steadfast in driving in the direction of the things that make you happy and leave you fulfilled. Beyond that, it's up to you. You can just ghost everyone if you don't mind burning bridges. You can meet with friends one-on-one and let them know what you're doing and why. You can even invite a friend to join you on your journey, although that usually doesn't work because it doesn't matter how much you want change for someone if they don't want it for themselves. People are ready to face uncomfort at different times, and some never are.

My preference is to build bridges instead of burn them. Make it clear and obvious to people which direction you're heading, and leave it up to them to cross the bridge and come with you. Most won't. That's not your problem. Just remember that you don't owe anyone anything more than honesty, compassion, and respect. Don't allow years of your life to pass you by waiting to cross the bridge yourself because you're afraid of hurting someone's feelings. Not everyone has dreams of inspiring the people around them, but if you do, it's imperative that you realize the importance of crossing that bridge. It could be the most impactful decision you ever make. You will inspire way more people by growing and continuing to level up than you ever will by putting your bus in park and remaining on the comfortable side of the bridge with everyone else.

One more thing: *Tension naturally wants to resolve.* The environment you're in right now doesn't want to change. It will resist, fight back, and try to sweet-talk you into returning to your old ways. It will try to tempt you back to the way things were. Don't look back. Decide confidently to never allow anyone to sit in the driver's seat of your bus, and accept that you must cross the bridge. Leverage the tension you've created and just keep moving forward.

MOMENTUM BUILDERS

NOW: Time for some "energy inventory." Make a list of ten people you currently spend the most time with. This can be friends, significant others, family, coworkers, workout buddies, and so on. Now, being brutally honest, label each person as one of the following: EE—energizing and encouraging, DD—draining and discouraging, ED—environment dependent, and AD—always draining.

TODAY: Figure out how to spend more time with the EE people because they are elevators for your life and heading in the same direction as you. With people who are DD, create clear boundaries because these people are clearly taking more than they are giving in your relationship and may be people you have to leave behind. Anyone with the label ED, figure out what environments make them value adds and what environments make them saboteurs, and limit your interactions to the former. Remove ADs from your life as quickly as possible before they demolish your dreams any further.

WELCOME TO EXCUSEVILLE

I was never a morning person. I thought I didn't have the right genetic profile or something to be able to get up at 5:00 a.m. ready to crush the day. While there is some biological basis to the circadian rhythm, the truth is that everyone is a morning person—most just have evening-person habits. Yup, that was me. I would mash the snooze button, sleep in, watch TV really late, and inevitably be exhausted when my alarm went off the next morning. As a result I was never at the gym when I said I would be, and I never got much done early in the day.

Here's the thing, though. Telling yourself you're not a morning person becomes a kind of self-fulfilling prophecy. If you're staying up past midnight scrolling your phone or watching Netflix, of course you're going to struggle to wake up early, get more done, and feel better about your goals. You're stuck in a cycle. There's even a phenomenon, introduced in a research paper published in 2014, called *bedtime procrastination.** That's when people deliberately put off going to bed so they can do whatever they want and engage in activities that they didn't have time for during the day. While people are aware of this deliberate self-sabotage, it unfortunately leads to serious daytime stress, sleepiness, and all sorts of other problems.

The issue, however, isn't sleep. It's *excuses*, the weaselly, bogus reasons we give ourselves and others for not doing what we know we're supposed to do so we don't have to feel guilty. To use a fitness example, people always ask me, "Brett, what's the best time to work out?" The answer is that there is no perfect time, but I respond with "What time would you prefer to work out?" A lot of people say they'd like to work out in the morning, but because it's hard for them to wake up and go to the gym, they'll say, "After work." Cool.

But here's what happens. Somebody vows to work out at 5:30 p.m. five days a week, but then on Monday, they work until 6:00 p.m. Tuesday is happy hour with colleagues. On Wednesday, they work late again. On Friday, a bunch of friends are going out to see their favorite band. And so on. What started out as a five-day workout pledge becomes *maybe* two workouts. The same thing happens week after week.

Deep down, you know when you're lying to yourself about your goals. You know when you're setting yourself up to find loophole after loophole. You just don't want to admit it. I see people do this all the time. They promise themselves that they're going to follow this rigorous plan, whether the goal is getting in shape, starting a business, saving money, working on their mental health, or starting or stopping any other habit. But they don't set themselves up for success. They don't change their

* Kroese, Floor M., Denise T. D. De Ridder, Catharine Evers, and Marieke A. Adriaanse. 2014. "Bedtime Procrastination: Introducing a New Area of Procrastination." *Frontiers in Psychology* 5 (611): 1–8. https://doi.org/10.3389/fpsyg.2014.00611.

environment. They don't recruit friends to help them resist temptation. They don't lay down any accountability structure. That guarantees they'll be making excuses for why they can't do what they just promised they would do.

Excuses always make sense to the person making them. They're fully committed to their excuse, which makes sense. The excuse is sparing them from feeling like a failure or admitting that they lied to themselves about their plan, so they cling to it. But that is a slippery slope. Tell yourself, "I can't stay fit because I don't have time" often enough and you'll not only start to believe it but also search out new ways to prove it's a fact. But it's just another lie. If I hired a private detective to follow you around during your day, I'll bet they would find hours every day that you're wasting that could be used to work out, meditate, take a personal finance course, or whatever you need to do to serve your goal. I'll wager I can find ninety wasted minutes in almost anyone's day.

Time, however, isn't the problem. It's *urgency.* You make excuses because, deep down, you think there will come a perfect time in the near future without distractions and time sucks, when you'll magically find total discipline and focus. Then, watch out!

That's another self-delusion. That time will never come. When you become comfortable believing your excuses, time passes, and you accomplish nothing. The reality is, you're never going to have a "this changes everything" epiphany; almost no one does. So stop waiting for one and making excuses to pass the time. Success is about putting yourself in the right place and frame of mind to take advantage of every opportunity to win the day, week, or month. To put it another way, if you want to catch a train, stand next to the tracks.

CALLING BULLSHIT

To get past excuse-making, stop telling yourself that excuses just happen. Every excuse has a reason behind it, as well as a lesson. For example, one of my excuses for not being "good" with money when I was younger was that I didn't know how much I had in my bank account. Why not? Because I was afraid to look at my balance and see how much I'd spent—and how little was left. I wasn't saving, and I wasn't educated in how to build wealth. It was money in, money out, not really thinking about it and spending way too much on the weekends and on small purchases here and there. I thought I was avoiding the uncomfort, but in reality I was living with the shame and anxiety of not knowing if the credit card would be over the limit or if my rent check would bounce.

Dig into why you make excuses. If you can't be on time for lunch with a certain person, maybe you don't actually respect that person's time because you're mad at them for some offense. If you constantly skip your workout on a given day, is it possible that you feel a bit embarrassed about not knowing how to use the equipment? Dig deep and find the reason because it's there. Until you are willing to face the *real* reason, you'll continue to validate that excuse.

THE LONGER YOU STAY, THE HARDER IT IS TO LEAVE

Excuses become problems when people choose the discomfort of comforting lies over the uncomfort of confronting the truth and making changes. You have the choice to play the victim card or be the victor. You have the choice to lean into and fight for all the reasons you can't do something or to educate yourself, try new things, and spend your time, money, and energy in ways that help you become a better version of yourself. Too many of us choose to hang out in *Excuseville.*

Excuseville looks like a great place because there is never a lack of company. But it's actually dangerous because those people will accept your excuses without question, and you'll accept theirs. You enable each other and don't hold each other accountable because you're all guilty of the same thing. You're not going to say, "We should be working out," because no one wants to be reminded of how they're lying to themselves and coming up short. Excuseville is built on a conspiracy of silence, not ruffling the feathers, and avoiding the pain of change.

The other thing about excuses is that nobody's neutral about them. For instance, I've found that high performers, the highly disciplined, and people who can't stand lame excuses don't like hanging out with people who make excuses all the time. If I'm supposed to meet you for lunch and you always have an excuse for why you're late or can't come, eventually, I'm going to lose patience and say, "Just tell me what the real reason is. Quit coming up with a story." Excuses are so toxic that they can wreck relationships. At some point they become the bullshit story you're telling yourself to avoid the uncomfortable side of growth. Disciplined people don't want to be around that for fear you might rub off on them.

That goes both ways. People who make excuses also don't like to be around people who get shit done because it makes them feel bad about themselves. That's why when you say, "I'm going to stop drinking," all your buddies who can't stop will protest, "Come on, you can have one beer." They will either try to sabotage you by tempting you to backslide to your old habit or get angry and drop the classic line: "You think you're better than us?"

This is why a big part of reaching your goals is escaping from Excuseville and the people in it. Hang with people who lift you up, not people who drag you down. Research from the Kellogg School found that if people in an office sat within twenty-five feet of a high performer, their own productivity increased by 15 percent. In contrast to that, people who sat next to an underperformer saw their own productivity decrease by *30* percent.* Woof. Discipline and apathy are both contagious, so it stands to reason that being around people who make excuses and never achieve anything can cause a performance decline. There aren't a lot of high performers walking around making excuses for all of their shortcomings. In fact, one of the prerequisites for being considered a high performer is ownership, which doesn't leave a lot of room for excuses.

To move past excuses, you're going to have to let some people down—your parents, family, friends, teachers. You'll have to unlearn some of the lessons other people taught you so you can do better. Consider that a test of loyalty. If the people who say they care about you really do, they'll be happy to see you grow. If not, you need to find better people to hang with. Time to pack up and get the hell out of Excuseville as soon as possible.

A BOULEVARD OF BROKEN PROMISES

Let's unpack what I mean by excuses. An excuse is a fabricated rationalization to explain to yourself (first) and others (second) why you can't keep a commitment. Some examples are as follows:

- I didn't have time.
- I'm too tired. (You need more sleep.)
- It's too time consuming.
- I can't afford that.
- I'm too busy.
- I've already made other plans.
- I forgot.
- I don't know what to do/say.

---

* Housman, Michael, and Dylan Minor. "Organizational Design and Space: The Good, the Bad, and the Productive." October 30, 2016. Harvard Business School Working Paper 16-147. Available at SSRN: https://ssrn.com/abstract=2805578 or http://dx.doi.org/10.2139/ssrn.2805578.

- I don't know where to start .
- I'm not ready.
- I never learned that.

My favorite is, "It's just not the right time." I hear this one when I'm talking with a client who's thinking about making a major life change, such as switching careers or starting a business. There's a reason every motivational speaker says there's no such thing as the right time: nobody got to where they are by waiting for someone to say, "Go!" You make it the right time. You stop waiting for the light at the end of the tunnel and trust yourself to walk alone in the dark. You make it the right time by embracing uncomfort and putting yourself in a situation to act—by creating an environment that makes it nearly impossible for you not to act and keep moving forward.

So many people believe that by waiting and delaying, they're sneakily avoiding uncomfort. But are they really? It's always better to pursue change on your own terms. It's much more uncomfortable to leave a job when you're forty-five and have two kids than when you're thirty and single. It's much more uncomfortable to start investing later in life after money is tight and you missed out on twenty years of compound interest. It's much more uncomfortable to start a fitness program after you have a heart attack than before you have one. When you make excuses, you're only delaying the uncomfort. I promise you, it's going to show up one way or the other.

Most excuses are as flimsy as a soap bubble. Back when I was doing fitness training, I had a rule: if you canceled a training session with less than three hours' notice, you would still be charged. When I first implemented this rule, I would give people one Get Out of Jail Free card. The second time, they would be charged. Now when someone forgot the second time, they inevitably had a dozen different excuses, all of which took away the responsibility for their bad planning or lack of commitment. They would text to let me know they couldn't make it, and I would say, "No problem, but just to remind you, I will have to charge you for the session." All of a sudden, I would get a message back: "Never mind, I'll be there." The excuse magically went out the window because there was a $75 payment attached to it. When there's a consequence, most excuses usually vanish. Some of the most effective consequences are financial. Nobody, and I mean nobody, likes to get hit in the wallet.

When you set goals and create a plan to meet them, you're making a promise to yourself. You're pledging to change bad habits and start new, productive ones. But each time you make an excuse and fail to do what you said you'd do, you break that promise. The more you make those excuses, the more you don't trust yourself. It's the same as having that friend who bails on you over and over again for lunch. After a few times sitting alone at a restaurant checking your watch, you stop trusting that person. When you betray your own trust enough times, you stop setting lofty goals and dreaming big because deep down you know you're lying to yourself. Your self-confidence wanes because you continue to break promises to yourself. This sabotages your self-belief, and eventually you stop setting goals at all, period.

Are you a liar? I think most people would immediately say no. Then why do you continually lie to yourself about what you're going to do? If you look for any reason not to keep your promises to yourself, eventually, you're going to turn fatalistic, convinced that you can't make changes, ever. That's when I hear people say things such as "I don't think I'll ever be able to get in shape" or "I think I'll die in debt." This is another time you'll hear "I've tried everything." You may have tried everything, but have you stuck with *anything*? If you can't trust yourself to do what's right, change becomes impossible. You lose any sense of your own integrity, and all that's left is shame.

UNCOMFORTABLE TRUTH NO. 5

"What you're not changing, you're choosing."

Dr. Laurie Buchanan is credited with that great quote, and she's right. Using an excuse more than once is making a choice to lie to yourself. Seriously.

Using an excuse once can be a defense mechanism against shame because you're not doing what you know you're supposed to be doing. But shame should be self-correcting. The next time you're supposed to work out or meet your partner at the couples therapist, you want to keep your promise because you don't want to feel that shame or embarrassment again.

If you continue to allow the same excuse, you're choosing this feeling, deliberately making yourself feel like crap.

Breaking this cycle is crucial to rebuilding your self-trust and self-confidence.

AVOID FUELING UP ON THE SPOTLIGHT EFFECT

One of the big reasons I see people making excuses is that they're comparing themselves to the ideals they see in the world around them, especially on social media. That's a huge source of shame. If you don't control what you see, hear, and read, you can develop a distorted perception of what other people are doing and wind up deepening your shame at not being as ripped as the guy on Facebook Reels or not owning five different lines of cosmetics like the celebrity on TikTok.

In fact, there's a messed-up mental process that plays out when you use other people's supposed accomplishments as an excuse for not stepping up and doing your work. First, you *compare*. You see someone doing handstand push-ups on YouTube and think that's the only acceptable level of fitness you can aspire to. You see someone showing off their eighty-foot yacht on Instagram and figure that's the standard if you want to feel successful. You're setting yourself up to fail before you've even begun.

Second, you start to *backpedal*. Faced with the reality that you'll probably never be as jacked as *Thor* actor Chris Hemsworth, you start to play down your goals and back away from them. You discredit potential aspirations by saying things such as "I wouldn't even want a six-pack or to be that muscular." Believing there's only one way to be in shape, build a rewarding career, or have a happy marriage is an example of distorted thinking. I used to do this with money by convincing myself that money was evil and saying things like, "I don't need money to be happy." I told myself comforting lies to avoid taking responsibility.

Finally, you *dismiss*. You convince yourself that everybody else has an easier circumstance than you. It's not fair because Chris Hemsworth has a personal trainer, a personal chef, and the time to work out eight hours a day, and if you had all those advantages . . . you see where I'm going with this? Every time you put someone on a pedestal and convince yourself that they have it easier than you, you lose. It does nothing to change your situation and just feeds your victim mentality.

Here's the truth. Even if people such as Chris Hemsworth or Jennifer Lopez have advantages, they still have to make good choices. Is J.Lo's chef following her around and slapping her wrist every time she goes to put M&Ms in her mouth? No, she still has to make a choice. If she wants to sneak into the bedroom and eat a bag of cookies under the covers, she can. She's choosing not to. If you're thinking, "Well, they get paid to be in shape, so it's easier for them," well, why haven't you ever connected the dots between your own health and fitness and your income? Can you say for sure that getting in the best shape of your life and showing up at work with better energy and confidence *won't* lead you to a raise or making more money?

Because I've seen this correlation over and over with clients, friends, and, yes, even with celebrities. The focus and discipline required to improve their fitness have led many of them to enjoy more career and relationship success and, yes, also make more money. This is not about privilege or advantages. This is about some people letting excuses run their life and other people saying, "No, I'm not going to lie to myself."

I don't care if you don't have a trainer or financial coach. You can still go for a walk, drink your bottle of water, or pay cash instead of using your credit card. None of those things are out of your control. But when you tell yourself stories—when you compare, backpedal, and dismiss—you're telling yourself that it's okay to make excuses because you'll never be perfect.

The empowering part of this is that you don't have to be perfect. The goal is progress, not perfection. Nobody is judging you or comparing you to the superheroes on social media. The belief that everyone else is scrutinizing your every move and waiting to laugh when you mess up is called the *spotlight effect.* It's what keeps people who are out of shape from going to the gym because they're self-conscious and ashamed. But let me tell you a secret. Do you know what all those people working out at the gym actually think about the out-of-shape guy who comes in to start his program? *Nothing.* They're paying attention to their own workouts and their own insecurities; they don't even notice the overweight man or woman—and if they do, more times than not, they'll be supportive, not mean. In every gym I've ever been in, the fittest guy in there is often the nicest and most encouraging. Because he understands how hard it is to show up day after day.

Want something you can do today, right now, that will help you reach your goals? Change your social media habits and quit comparing yourself with every Pilates goddess and jet-flying billionaire who makes you feel "less than." Why? First, because you don't know their backstory or what their *behind the scenes* looks like. Second, because for everyone who seems like a superstar, there are a hundred people reaching exactly the kind of goals you want to reach and being thrilled about it. You don't need to be a superhero or a billionaire to be insanely healthy, happy, fit, and successful. You do, however, need to be accountable for your own life and stop allowing the spotlight effect to fuel your excuses.

HOME OF THE BISON

All the advice I'm giving you about excuses comes down to the following two things:

1. Being aware of how often you're making excuses and which ones you're using
2. Figuring out what uncomfort you're avoiding by relying on excuses and breaking your promises to yourself

Think about the three excuses you've used most often in the last six months and what they're helping you avoid. Are you dodging your workout? Eating right? Going to counseling with your partner? Finally leaving your job? Relocating? Ending a bad relationship? Having to spend time alone with yourself?

Next, what do you think would happen if you went one week without using those excuses and instead followed through on what you promised yourself you would do? This No-Excuses Week is something anyone can do. You can do anything for seven focused days!

Finally, what's the uncomfort you should be leaning into that you've been avoiding with excuses instead? Shame? Guilt? Fear of failure? Fear of confronting some past trauma? Fear of success? The belief that maybe you don't have what it takes to reach your goals, even if you go all in? If you go on a one-week "excuse cleanse," I guarantee you'll find that the uncomfort you're avoiding is a lot less painful than the shame of lying to yourself again and again.

If you learn to run toward uncomfort, you'll be amazed at how fast you'll stop relying on excuses. Here's a way to think about it. When cattle are out in the field and they sense a storm coming, their instincts tell them to run away from it. Of course, the storm finally catches up to them, and when it does, they're caught in it for much longer because they're moving in the same direction as the storm.

On the other hand, when bison see that a storm is coming, their instincts are the opposite. They turn and run *toward* it. As a result they don't avoid the storm, but because they're taking the uncomfortable head-on course, the storm passes over them a lot faster than it does for the cows. Which will you be, a cow or a bison?

Ignoring the issue, distracting yourself, and continuing to seek comfort won't make your problems better. It will make your problems *bigger.* Avoiding something means you live with it a lot longer, because the situation never fixes itself. But if you turn and run toward it, as scary as that can be, you blunt its power. That comes with progress and confidence, not excuses.

MOMENTUM BUILDERS

NOW: Take a moment to write down the three most common excuses you use and what you are avoiding by using these excuses. This reflection will help you call these excuses out when you go to use them again. When that happens, move as quickly as you can to take the action and avoid using that excuse again.

TODAY: Begin to restrict, unfollow, or block any social media accounts you currently follow that cause you to negatively compare yourself, discourage you, or fuel your excuses for not keeping your own promises to yourself. Be ruthless. If the first feeling you get when you come across their content is negative, unfollow. There is a big difference between tough love that lights a fire under your ass and disempowering content that makes you feel like shit.

CHAPTER 6

THE THREE CONFIDENCE CRIMINALS

In the last chapter, we explored one of the unfortunate mental habits that can derail you on your way to change: excuses. In this one we'll dig into another set of joy-stealing, potential-derailing bad guys. I call them Confidence Criminals.

It's hard to overstate the importance of the role that confidence plays in the journey from who you are to who you want to become. Confidence is the belief that you'll keep the promises you made to yourself back when you set your goals and made your plan. It's the certainty that you have what it takes to get up early, work late, change your environment, adopt new habits, and do whatever it takes to win. Just as important, confidence is also the belief that if you screw up or blow off your plan for a day, you'll get right back to it the next day. It's trusting yourself.

Confidence Criminals undermine the belief that you've got this. They sabotage you by instilling doubt, like a little cartoon devil perched on your shoulder and whispering in your ear, "You can't do this. You suck. You've already failed multiple times to get it done. Why should this time be any different?" I've already talked about the fact that an excuse is a broken promise to yourself; Confidence Criminals are the psychological terrorists that are most likely to make you break that promise. The following are the three Confidence Criminals:

1. Limiting Beliefs
2. Impostor Syndrome
3. Perfectionism

Confidence is the key to handling uncomfort. When you do what some of my former clients have done and leave your job to chase the dream of becoming an entrepreneur or a solopreneur, you have to have some confidence in your ability. Nobody would leave their job if they thought they were bad at what they do, right? But because you're human, you're always walking a tightrope between "I *know* I can do it" and "I *hope* I can do it." There's always a little self-doubt, which can be healthy in small doses. Self-doubt, when used correctly, prevents us from becoming complacent and lazy.

What we don't want is for self-doubt to fester and become overwhelming. That's why this chapter is so important. It's critical to recognize when the Confidence Criminals have broken into your brain and are causing you to lose faith in yourself. That way, you can push back. I think about the kid standing on the edge of a diving board. You've done that, right? It doesn't look like much from the pool deck, but when you get up there, twelve feet feels like the top of a twelve-story building. You'll see a kid there, shaking and saying, "I can't do this." That's most of us at one time or another when it comes to facing uncomfort. We all have those moments of crippling self-doubt.

But if you understand the Confidence Criminals and how they can derail you, you can shut them up long enough that you're able to jump off the diving board. Then what happens? You fall, going, "Oh shiiiiiiit!" and hit the water, and then you kick back to the surface, realize you're still alive, and what was fear now feels like an exhilarating rush of adrenaline, like you just hit a game-winning homer in the World Series. Fear has been replaced with confidence. Wait a minute—you *can* do this. And now you're running to get in line to do it again. We'll talk about confidence a lot in this part of the book, but it all starts here.

Now let's take a closer look at the Confidence Criminals, see what the source of their power is, and discover how you can render them powerless to stop you.

LIMITING BELIEFS

There are many kinds of limiting beliefs, but the ones I see most often are the beliefs that turn doubts into self-fulfilling prophecies. Those beliefs are either stories that people hold on to or patterns of thinking that are disempowering. The stories turn temporary outcomes into permanent conclusions, such as "I've never been a runner," or "No one ever taught me how to start a business." They write this story onto their tombstone in a weird way and presume that things will never change. But we change all the time. Life forces us to learn new things, move, or start a new job. Nothing is ever final as long as you're willing to try, to embrace the uncomfort.

The patterns of thinking are even more dangerous. They're part of what the great psychologist Dr. Martin Seligman calls "learned helplessness." People who fall victim to learned helplessness tend to think about failure or setbacks as personal, pervasive, and permanent. For example:

- **Personal:** "I didn't stick to my diet because I have no willpower."
- **Pervasive:** "I always fail when it comes to discipline."
- **Permanent:** "I'm never going to be able to lose weight."

This could be someone who fails to finish a "couch to 5K" training program and blames herself, lets the failure spiral, and decides she'll never run a 5K and quits. Forget about the extenuating circumstances of why she failed or the fact that she has a support system that will allow her to try again. She's decided she's helpless in the face of forces beyond her control, and she might never get back on the horse. That's a tragedy.

Limiting beliefs drain your power and delude you into thinking you lack some essential quality that other people possess, such as concluding that Chris Hemsworth is jacked only because he has some genetic X factor that you lack. Either that or, even worse, we convince ourselves that the people who do achieve big things just got "lucky." That's a poisonous dead end because it removes everything that you have control over from the equation: planning, environment, discipline, mindset.

Your default needs to be to assume that other people worked their ass off for what they have and instead ask yourself, "Am I willing to do the same?"

A former business coach of mine once said, "Brett, what is the difference between you and Tony Robbins?" I answered with "I don't know, a thriving business and a billion dollars?" He said, "No, time and reps. He's been doing it for longer, and because of those reps, he has more experience and confidence in what he does, and that's it." There are a hundred ways to achieve any goal, from getting fit to starting a small business. Just because you didn't get there the same way as someone else doesn't mean you can't get there. But if that belief prevents you from ever trying again, it doesn't matter. You've already lost.

How do you take the power away from limiting beliefs? By confronting them and questioning them. One version of this is what Dr. Seligman calls "learned optimism," and it's the flip side of learned helplessness. You make failures impersonal, isolated, and incidental.

- **Impersonal:** "I quit my diet because I didn't get rid of all the temptations in my environment."
- **Isolated:** "Just because I blew it with my diet today doesn't mean I can't still hit my workout and drink plenty of water."
- **Incidental:** "Next time, with a little more focus and some extra accountability, I will be successful."

You can hear the difference in those statements, right? They're empowering. They don't turn one failure into some sort of half-assed verdict from the universe. You're no longer talking about what you can't do but about how you'll find a way to do better when you get back on the horse. When you're planning and strategizing, you're already playing to win. That's being on offense instead of defense. You're moving from limiting beliefs to "limitless belief."

CALLING BULLSHIT

Among the million self-appointed gurus and experts on the internet, few are worse than the ones who insist that you can have a great body, perfect health, or overflowing wealth with no pain or sacrifice (usually using their secret $99 shortcut). Those folks are great at targeting people who want results and change while remaining comfortable. There is no lasting, real change without sacrifice and hard work. You have to give up some part of who you were to become who you want to be. You have to lift the weights or cut up your credit cards. Anyone who tells you that change is possible without requiring you to actually change anything is selling you a big ol' can of BS.

IMPOSTOR SYNDROME

Remember how I got injured during my junior year in high school? Well, it sucked. I had been a three-sport athlete, and now I was in street clothes on the bench. But we also had this thing at my school called the Pops Concert. It was like a Broadway musical for our high school, with singing, dancing, and it was a big deal. I had always thought acting would be fun, but until now sports had taken up most of my time. I decided to use my current situation as an opportunity to do that show in my senior year. After having sports taken away, I wanted to be part of something. If I wasn't going to play quarterback for the New York Giants, my fallback was to be Leonardo DiCaprio.

However, to do the Pops Concert, you had to take choir for the full year. I wasn't super keen on taking choir because while I actually enjoyed singing, I was not comfortable or confident singing in front of other people. I would much rather flex my golden pipes alone in my car or shower. But this was the requirement I faced. Plus, I wanted to challenge myself. Remember, I had been the quarterback, the stud athlete, and like most schools, at my school the jocks and the arts students didn't have much crossover.

On the first day of my senior year, choir was the only class I was nervous about. I remember walking into the choir room, and I was petrified. I hadn't told anyone about my participation in choir, and for the first time in a while, I felt like an outsider. I felt like a loser. I felt like the person who didn't know what was going on. After a brief silence, someone at the back of the room (I don't know who) yelled, "You're in the wrong room."

Everybody knew I wasn't supposed to be there. Nobody in our school who played football or basketball did choir. Except that I was actually signed up for choir. I scanned the room for an empty chair, sat down, and assumed all those singers, who actually knew what was going on, were talking about me behind my back. It was an unwanted reminder of what it was like to have no confidence about something. But what I'm really proud of is that I started to make friends in that room and to build my confidence back up. People started saying, "Maybe this isn't a joke to him. I guess he's serious."

I wasn't a great singer. But the kids in that room started to take me under their wings and teach me things. By the end of the year, not only did I lock down the third leading role (as Hatch Lumberjack) in the school play, but there were also two other football players who transferred into choir because I opened the door for them a little. All of a sudden, we were part of the Pops Concert. Plus, I gained a whole new group of friends that I probably would never have gotten to know because I thought we didn't have anything in common.

So that's my *Glee* moment, but there is a point to it. When I walked into that choir room, my impostor syndrome almost made me walk out. Impostor syndrome is defined as feeling anxious about whether you belong in a group or whether you deserve to be seen as a success. Basically, you feel like a fraud, and you're sure that at any moment, you'll be exposed, and everyone will start laughing at you. Even people who are high-performing by any objective definition fall victim to impostor syndrome. It shows up at every level.

I think the basic impulse behind impostor syndrome is a healthy one. You should be putting yourself into uncomfortable situations on the regular because you're trying new things and growing. That's what I call "curiosity over complacency." It's great to seek out novel experiences that push you into unfamiliar territory. But if you can only frame unfamiliar experiences in terms of who's better than you, impostor syndrome will eat you alive. I could become the most well-known coach and speaker in the world and still never be as well known as Tony Robbins. So what? Comparison can't be the measuring stick that decides what targets you decide to pursue. According to research, between 56 and 82 percent of college students, nurses, medical students, and other professionals feel like frauds from time to time.* The symptoms of the syndrome are no joke and can include anxiety, depression, burnout, exhaustion, avoidance of demanding tasks, and the rejection of positive feedback.

Are you on social media a lot? That just makes the problem worse. Platforms such as TikTok, Instagram, and LinkedIn tend to exacerbate this because everybody shares their "living the dream" stories or their #blessed photo essays. They don't show themselves wrist-deep in a pint of Ben & Jerry's or getting rejected at job interviews, so it's easy to conclude that everyone but you is crushing life. Impostor syndrome makes us feel almost unworthy to be seeking excellence or achievement because we're not good enough to deserve it. In fact, we treat obstacles as evidence that we really are impostors—the "See, I told you so" effect.

Curious people don't conclude without evidence that they can't do something. They ask open-ended questions: What skills would I have to learn? How much would I have to invest? What would I have to do? What would I sell? What would that business look like? The more questions you ask, the more the world opens up and what had felt impossible now starts to appear very doable.

For example, I currently have a buddy who recently completed an impressive thirty-mile desert trail run. I was sitting on the beach with him when he shared this idea with me for the first time. He told me he'd been running out in the desert in Arizona, where he lived, and he wondered if there were any trail records for the path he often ran. He did some research and found a few trail records, some of which he thought he might be able to break.

---

* Bravata, D. M., S. A. Watts, A. L. Keefer, D. K. Madhusudhan, K. T. Taylor, D. M. Clark, R. S. Nelson, K. O. Cokley, and H. K. Hagg. "Prevalence, Predictors, and Treatment of Impostor Syndrome: a Systematic Review." *J Gen Intern Med* 35, no. 4 (2020): 1252-1275. https://doi.org/10.1007/s11606-019-05364-1. Epub 2019 Dec 17. PMID: 31848865; PMCID: PMC7174434.

That might have been the end of the conversation for some people, but together we kept asking questions and going deeper and deeper. What would it take both physically and mentally to run that far? How long would it take? What's the farthest he's ever run? We kept going, and fifteen questions later, it actually didn't seem that impossible. Now the only question was: Was he willing to train and do all the work it takes to run thirty miles? He said he was.

Whether he set the new trail record isn't even the point. It's the fact that after fifteen minutes of open-minded and curious questions, his impostor syndrome decreased significantly. The minute he started to train for this race, his impostor syndrome continued to dissipate until it vanished completely and was replaced by confidence.

Battling impostor syndrome begins with finding ways to focus your sense of worth on internal metrics and, frankly, not giving a shit about what other people think of you—on giving more weight to what you've achieved so far than on the opinions of others. You can also dismiss impostor syndrome as a perfectly natural response to moving into uncomfort, which it is. Who wouldn't feel some doubt in unfamiliar company or among people who are more accomplished? If you frame the situation in a healthy way, you might conclude that you have something to learn from people who've done what you aspire to do!

Another way to beat impostor syndrome is to ignore the shallow, materialistic measures of achievement in favor of things that can't be quantified. If you look hard enough (and sometimes, you don't even have to look that hard), you can always find someone who's accomplished more than you have—run more miles, made more money, impacted more people, and so on. But if you base your sense of self-worth and accomplishment on things that can't be quantified, such as helping other people, learning new skills, walking into rooms with great energy, or challenging your own limits, you'll always come out ahead.

Coaches and speakers feel impostor syndrome all the time. After all, we're expected to teach someone how to change their lives! But we understand that the feeling of being a fraud is transient. All we need is to be one step ahead of someone in our area of expertise to help them improve. I don't have to be the fittest, most successful, most disciplined person of all time, but at my level of experience and knowledge, I could certainly help somebody else improve their mindset, discipline, and confidence.

I'd rather view impostor syndrome as an earned badge of honor because if you're trying new things and putting yourself out there, of course you will feel uncomfortable. Congratulations, you're living life! The bigger problem comes if you never feel impostor syndrome at all because that means you're playing it too small.

Framed in the right way, impostor syndrome can be a positive. If you get a promotion at your job, it's because your bosses see that you're ready for a new role. But you've never been in that role, with a new title, new status, and new expectations. Of course you're going to feel some impostor syndrome, but it comes with something you really wanted. The trick is to understand that it's fleeting and get about the business of proving to yourself that you deserve it.

UNCOMFORTABLE TRUTH NO. 6

Learn from the past—don't live there.

Human beings have this unfortunate tendency to punish ourselves for the choices we made in the past, which are, by definition, things we can't change. This regretful self-shaming contributes to impostor syndrome by making us feel like we might *not* have been a fraud if only we had known then what we know now, if only we had chosen door no. 2 instead of door no. 1.

The solution? Extend yourself a little grace. Accept this powerful truth: five years ago, or last week, you were doing the best you could based on what you knew and who you were at the time. That's it. We all do the best we can, even if at the time, it sucks. Nobody gets up and says, "I'm gonna go make a decision that will screw up my life today!" You can't change the past, so be kind and learn from it so you can do better tomorrow.

PERFECTIONISM

Perfectionism and impostor syndrome are closely linked. In a way, perfectionism is the dysfunctional core for impostor syndrome because if you feel like a fraud, all you have to do is perform perfectly, and you've proven to everyone that you're not, right? Unfortunately, the only one whose opinion matters is you, and if you're lost in perfectionism, nothing is ever good enough.

That's what perfectionism is really all about. Whatever you do is never good enough. Perfectionism says that success is a binary thing: either you succeed 100 percent or you're a total failure. There's no in-between. That's the sort of high-pressure mental model I see in students who can't tolerate the idea of getting a B in a class and would rather risk cheating than getting a lower grade on their own merits. That's a recipe for stress, burnout, and hating what you do.

Every so often a potential client will tell me they're an "all in" type of person, thinking that sounds good and will make me excited to work with them. But I'll reply, "When you tell me that you're an all-in person, that's also telling me that there will be periods of time that you're going to be all out. An all-in mentality is good for speed and intensity, but it's often counterproductive for consistency." Yes, being all in on your desire to change should be nonnegotiable. However, when it comes to building momentum, perfectionism often does more harm than good.

Perfectionism is the hare in the old fable. Consistency is the tortoise. While the hare might have some flashes when he's going all in, he's going to have even more periods when he's slacking, distracted, or giving up because of impostor syndrome. Meanwhile, the tortoise keeps going—not flashy, not perfect, but always chugging along. At the end of the story, it's the tortoise that wins the race.

Yes of course, there are plenty of other scenarios I could mention where being the hare would be beneficial; I'm not here to take away your strengths. If one of your strengths is going all in on something or working in short bursts of intensity, that's great. But what that line usually means is that you're all in when something's fun and exciting, when everything is set up properly, and when you're seeing top-notch results. But when that honeymoon phase ends—when you have a cheat day or miss a milestone or life just gets complicated—that all-in perfectionist mentality tells me you're more likely to start beating yourself up and doing what I call "hitting the 'Fuck It' button." (More to come on this "fun" little button later.)

Perfectionism often comes from growing up or existing in an environment with rigid, high expectations, critical or shaming parents, or excessive praise for your achievements, which in your mind linked the love you received to your accomplishments. But with the right shift in mindset, that kind of thinking can easily be turned into an asset. I'll sometimes tell perfectionist clients, "Unless this is the NFL or NBA and we have a six-month offseason, we need to find a way to keep you going year-round. Because you probably can't take six months off from running your business or hitting the gym, right?"

Then I'll work with them on downshifting. If they have a gear where they can go fast and intense for weeks or months, great. Let's use that and bank some big results. Then when the results start to drop, conditions change, or the cold, dark months of winter come around, instead of slamming the parking brake, what if we just slowed down?

This means reframing success as gradual progress, not massive leaps. Thinking in terms of massive leaps leads to disappointment because those leaps require huge changes that are hard to sustain. But if you work out and eat well enough to average a five-hundred-calorie deficit per day, do you know how much weight you'll lose in a year? About fifty pounds. If you deposited $20 into a savings account paying 5 percent interest every day for three years, you'd end up with $23,651. I'll bet you spend more than that right now every day on Starbucks and Amazon!

Showing up is perfect. Making any small progress is perfect. Later in this book, you're going to see me talk about "wins" a lot—win the morning, win the day, Never Miss a Monday, the importance of small wins, things like that. There's a reason. You will never be perfect. I will never be perfect. The awesome thing is, we don't have to be.

As good as it sounds to be all in, I much prefer the mentality of *no zero days*. Checking every commitment off your list and hitting 100 percent won't positively impact your progress as much as a zero day, where you don't follow through on any of your commitments, will negatively affect it. Just for good measure, let me repeat that:

A zero day will diminish your progress far more than a perfect day will enhance it.

Aiming for more good days and trying to limit your terrible days can lead to fantastic results at the end of a year—*as long as you keep showing up*. As long as you learn to give yourself credit—to love yourself and be proud of yourself—for showing up and winning the day. This isn't the World Series or the US Open. There isn't one winner and a bunch of losers. Progress is the only outcome that matters.

So how do you get past those perfectionist tendencies?

- **Practice self-kindness.** Be nice to yourself, including changing your self-talk. Negative self-talk is corrosive because your brain hears what comes out of your mouth and believes it. I'm not talking about empty affirmations; I'm talking about giving yourself a high five for what you did right during the day, not berating yourself for what you didn't get to. Nobody likes a Negative Nancy or Condescending Carl. So don't let them live in your head either.
- **Question your goals and expectations.** Is what you're demanding from yourself realistic? Or are you putting so much pressure on yourself that you're bound to fail, trapping you in a shame cycle of big expectations and inevitable failures? If so, it's time to think about setting goals and targets that still push you but don't require you to be superhuman. Make sure that when you feel more like Clark Kent, you're still able to succeed.
- **Redefine success.** Is it only about the number on the scale or in the bank? Or is it about feeling energetic, having peace of mind, and keeping the ball moving down the field? Remember, a home run that travels 550 feet and one that barely clears the fence both only count for one run.
- **No zero days.** What are two or three daily tasks or commitments that equal a great day in your health, work, or relationships? While hitting all those every day would be

great, how can you avoid any zero days? Any day that's not a zero means that even if you're slowing down, you're still moving forward.

Let's close with a bonus uncomfortable truth: perfectionism is *not* a virtue. **Perfectionism is just a fancy, low-hanging excuse that feels like a compliment.** Being honest with yourself about things like that is how you'll lock up the Confidence Criminals for good.

MOMENTUM BUILDERS

NOW: Analyze the goals you haven't reached yet and determine which of the Confidence Criminals has been your biggest enemy: limiting beliefs, impostor syndrome, or perfectionism. Now rewrite a brand-new statement for yourself that is encouraging and built around confidence.

TODAY: Establish the three to five daily personal commitments that make up a great day for you. Get clear on what internal or external factors could affect you and potentially force you into a zero day. Now start early and often and put all your emphasis into checking at least one of these personal commitments off your list within the first ninety minutes of your day. Once you do, you can celebrate the momentum that enabled you to avoid having a zero day.

PART III

SETTING GOALS YOU'LL ACTUALLY ACCOMPLISH

THE SEVEN COMMON GOAL-SETTING MISTAKES

I have a love-hate relationship with long-term goals. It's great to have a long-term vision and a North Star, but so many people set the goal, pack it away in a notebook somewhere, put it in their desk, and just assume that over a year or two, it's magically going to come true. But goals with a deadline that far away lack one of the biggest driving factors for taking action and creating change: *urgency.* If there's no urgency to change and no urgency to stay disciplined, then there's no urgency that defines why today matters or this week matters. It's easy to kick the can down the road.

When I work with people, it's not that we don't set long-term goals; we do. But we put 80–90 percent of our focus on short-term goals of ninety days or less. That's a time horizon people can understand. You can visualize what will be happening ninety days from now. More importantly, a period like ninety days is short enough to create a sense of *time scarcity*, the sense that every day matters. It's easier to create urgency because what you do today matters. What you do this week matters. If your goal doesn't make you feel like today matters, it's too far away. Set a leveraged goal with a shorter deadline. Also, long-term goals depend on you hitting short-term goal after short-term goal, so that's where more of your focus should be.

Goals are deeply, deeply misunderstood. People talk about goal setting like it's some sort of magical incantation, but it's not. In 2019 Strava, the company that makes the popular running and cycling app, found that by the second Friday of January, 80 percent of New Year's resolution makers had said, "Screw it."* That wouldn't happen if goal setting was some guarantee of success. It's not, but not for the reasons you might think. If you're setting goals but never reaching them, it's not because you don't have the ability to hit goals. It's because you're setting the wrong goals in the wrong way. In this chapter I'm going to teach you how to fix that by helping you avoid the seven most common goal-setting mistakes.

GOAL MISTAKE NO. 1: CONFUSING GOAL SETTING WITH TAKING ACTION

Many people think setting a goal equals *doing something.* It's January 2, everybody's got their goals set, and there's this huge dopamine rush. They're all thinking, "I'm going to crush this year!" It's not that I think everybody's completely full of shit; they really do want this to be a transformative year. But wanting it isn't enough. You can't set a goal and then go back to bed and expect a few declarations on a piece of paper to manifest on their own.

Setting a goal gives you a vision to shoot for, but the only way to get there is through deliberate and consistent action. If you're setting a goal

* Haden, Jeff. "A Study of 800 Million Activities Predicts Most New Year's Resolutions Will Be Abandoned on January 19: How to Create New Habits That Actually Stick." Inc.com. January 3, 2020. https://www.inc.com/jeff-haden/a-study-of-800-million-activities-predicts-most-new-years-resolutions-will-be-abandoned-on-january-19-how-you-cancreate-new-habits-that-actually-stick.html.

that requires a massive change, you have to change your environment. You have to change your schedule. You have to ask for help where you need it. You need to get rid of any friction that's stopping you from taking action.

GOAL MISTAKE NO. 2: SETTING VAGUE GOALS

Let's say one of your goals is to "eat healthier." That seems great in theory, but I have questions. Does that mean at every meal? Does that mean a salad first thing in the morning? Does that mean all three meals or just two? Where will you get the healthy food? What *is* healthy food? Will you order it online or go to the grocery store? Will you make it at home or order it from a restaurant? If it's the store, when do you go? Also, what types of healthy food? Apples? Bananas? Vegetables? Lean proteins? What's in season? What if you begin to crave dessert? What if you're eating out with friends? What if it's your birthday or a holiday? Is anybody else in your family going to eat healthy, or is it just you?

You see where I'm going with this. I'm not just being annoying. I'm asking legit questions that are all but certain to show up for you. If you don't answer these questions now, you will face these types of decisions every day, which will lead to you feeling overwhelmed and confused. You'll wind up with decision fatigue, and you'll often choose the fastest and easiest option, regardless of your goal. A vague goal leaves you constantly improvising, which means on a given day, there are dozens of ways you can drop the ball.

Instead, ask and answer all the critical questions up front. Get black-and-white answers with zero gray area. The more scenarios you can envision, the more plans and resources you can have in place to help you do what you need to do. For example:

- I will add fruit to my first and second meals and rotate between an apple and strawberries.

- I will order enough fruit, vegetables, and lean meats so I can eat at home five nights a week.
- I will order from my two favorite healthy restaurants on Tuesdays and Fridays.
- I will shop at Trader Joe's every Sunday around 6:00 p.m. as part of my "Sunday Setup."
- I will cut and refrigerate all of my fruit on Mondays so it's easy to grab on the way to work.

And so on. Now you just have to follow through. If you have to answer a dozen questions just to follow through any given day, and you're already tired or frustrated, that's enough reason to say, "To hell with it. I'll do it tomorrow." That brings up a really important idea that I want to share with you.

Reaching your goals is about minimizing friction.

I wrote about friction earlier when I talked about changing your environment. But there's more to reducing friction. Work, longtime habits, inconveniences, commitments, being disorganized—they all increase friction in your life, making it harder for you to do what's already difficult, which is to *change*. By going into the goal-setting process with your eyes open, you can anticipate the areas of potential friction and minimize them as much as possible.

Hate going to the grocery store? Have groceries delivered. Intimidated by investing? Use an app that invests money for you automatically. Instead of going straight into execution after you set your goal, *organize*. Organize your thoughts, your requirements, your supplies and equipment, your consequences, and even what happens when you screw up and miss a day anyway. If you've planned ahead and anticipated the roadblocks that are going to come up, you enter the game with a much higher chance of winning. This is the perfect example of choosing to answer the hard questions now so your life can be easier later on.

GOAL MISTAKE NO. 3: AVOIDING EXTERNAL ACCOUNTABILITY AND CONSEQUENCES

Goals are good, but commitments are better. A commitment is a goal with consequences attached. How can you turn your goals into commitments? You find ways to attach consequences to the times when you procrastinate or get lazy and don't do what you're supposed to do.

If you're trying to achieve outcomes you've never been able to achieve before, you need a higher level of accountability too. If you blow off something you need to do to make progress and nothing happens, you'll just do it again. You need to set up multiple layers of accountability and consequences to keep yourself on the path. My former policy of charging my fitness training clients if they canceled less than three hours before a lesson is one example. Here are others:

- Pay a mental health therapist in advance and lose the money if you don't show up.
- Join a support group (a writers' group, a workout group) that requires hitting weekly milestones and doesn't let members participate unless they do the work. For example, if you don't submit a chapter of your in-progress book, you can't join the weekly team call.
- Link goals to an important event on the calendar that puts some pressure on you and can't be pushed back, such as a doctor's appointment or class reunion.

Goals treat change as a matter of willpower. It's not. This is what I call the *sailboat fallacy*. People who don't sail assume that getting from point A to point B is a matter of setting the course, steering the boat in that direction, and being patient. But sailing isn't that simple. The wind changes direction, and currents can push you off course. Sailors know you have to tack and jibe and make a hundred course corrections before you can arrive at a safe harbor. That's what setting and reaching goals is like. If you're smart, you assume there will be obstacles that threaten your goals, so you're prepared for them. Goals are never "set and forget."

CALLING BULLSHIT

There's a cliché that writing your goals down makes you more likely to achieve them. But what does science say about that? Well, a study done at Dominican University in 2007 found that people who wrote their goals down achieved substantially more than those who did not.* But that's not law-of-attraction magic. Neurologists found that writing goals down means you remember them better. It's not surprising that if you can recall something in detail, you're in better shape to work through it and knock it off your to-do list. Plus, you're more likely to see what you wrote and be reminded of your goals. But writing your goals out by itself accomplishes nothing. So write all you want, but use that list to take action and get moving. That's where the real magic lies.

* Gardner, Sarah, and Dave Albee. "Study Focuses on Strategies for Achieving Goals, Resolutions." 2015. https://scholar.dominican.edu/cgi/viewcontent.cgi?article=1265&context=news-releases.

GOAL MISTAKE NO. 4: WANTING THE RESULT BUT HATING THE PROCESS

You can't just love the result because that could be months or years away. If you're going to get there, you have to enjoy the climb, including the parts where you're uncomfortable. If somebody says, "I want to lose twenty pounds," that's exciting because eventually, they're going to look in the mirror and be leaner. But it also makes them nervous because they have to order different food when they go out to eat or go to the gym where they're self-conscious. That combination of excitement and a little bit of fear creates exhilaration, which leads to that dopamine hit we get when we do hard things.

Another example of this is my client who wanted to grow his real estate company by 50 percent. He said, "God, if I can do this, it would change my confidence, my company, my family, everything." He really wanted to hit that number. But it also scared the shit out of him because he had to hire people, which meant he had to commit capital and lead a team, which was way out of his comfort zone.

There's an old saying that goes, "The best workout is the one you'll do," meaning we're more likely to do what excites us. That's true. In setting your goals, follow the 75/25 rule: Set a goal that excites you 75 percent of the time. The other 25 percent of the time, you should be leaning into the uncomfort and feeling nervous—or even scared—about what it's going to take to accomplish the goal. This is the correct ratio. This is how you fall in love with the process of change, not just the outcome.

Change is supposed to be a little scary. We keep growing because we keep doing uncomfortable things. Your process, the steps you need to take to get to your goal, should always have that 75 percent mix of exciting and positive blended with 25 percent uncomfort. That way, every day, as you go through each stage, you're getting that adrenaline rush that comes with pushing yourself and doing what used to scare you.

UNCOMFORTABLE TRUTH NO. 7

You've wasted so much time looking for the next shortcut when the fastest way is to just do the damn work.

Like it or not, there are rules to follow and work you'll have to embrace if you want to get optimal results from choosing uncomfort. They are as follows:

- You must change your current environment. Your current environment is set up to keep you the same. If you want to change, start with your environment. For example, you can't hang out with people who sabotage and talk you out of your commitments, no matter how much they seem like good friends. You can't fill your house with junk food and expect to lose weight. You can't sit on the couch and watch TV every night if you have unfinished daily commitments. This will suck at first, but it's a must.
- Follow advice from the book *Atomic Habits*: Set yourself up for what you can do on your worst day, not your best day. If you expect to crush it every day, the minute you don't, you'll get discouraged. Instead, set a high floor, and even when you can only manage the minimum, you'll have made progress.
- You'll confront your past failures, not so you can feel bad about them but so you can identify what tripped you up and avoid it. I call this "watching game film." The goal is to avoid making the same mistakes multiple times in a row.
- You will screw up and get back on the horse. A slipup isn't failure; that's being human. Failure is getting comfortable with losing. When did we let that happen? *Do not* allow yourself to become numb to losing.

Commit to your new plan for a minimum of ninety days because that's a "real life" time frame. It allows for things to happen—work, travel, holidays, injuries, family emergencies—so you're forced to adapt to them and prove you can be consistent over time.

GOAL MISTAKE NO. 5: SETTING YOUR GOALS BASED ON OTHERS' EXPECTATIONS

It's easy to fall into the trap of pursuing goals that reflect what *others*—parents, peers, society—deem important. You might be influenced by social norms, celebrities, or the expectations voiced by family or friends. There are two problems with this. First, it often leads to a lack of engagement and motivation because they're not *your* goals. Second, when you find yourself achieving targets that were never directly aligned to your happiness or fulfillment, you can feel regret instead of exhilaration. Here are some examples:

- **Career Choices:** You pursue a law or medical degree to satisfy your parents' desire to see you in a prestigious profession despite having a strong passion for another field.
- **Lifestyle Goals:** You buy a large house or expensive car because your social circle values material success. This could lead to financial strain and a sense of being trapped by possessions that offer little personal joy.
- **Partner Decisions:** You decide to marry the safe choice that all your friends and family deem to be a "nice guy" instead of trusting your own heart and listening to your intuition that it's not the right fit.

It's crucial to choose goals rooted in your personal values and long-term vision. This requires introspection—and oftentimes the courage to diverge from the path others have envisioned for you. This is as important for your goals this year as it is for your full vision for your life. Start by clearly defining your long-term vision. This should encapsulate not only what you want to achieve but also *who you want to become*. It might include the kind of work-life balance you want, the values you want to live by, and the impact you'd like to have on the world. Each goal you set should be a stepping stone toward this vision. For example, if your vision includes being an influential writer, your goals might involve writing daily, publishing articles regularly, and networking with other writers and editors.

Your personal vision will probably evolve over time, so it's important to periodically reassess your goals to ensure they remain aligned with who you're becoming. Taking ownership of your goals will increase your motivation and satisfaction. Also, when others know about your vision and the reasons behind your goals, they're more likely to support your efforts, even if you're diverging from their expectations.

GOAL MISTAKE NO. 6: WORDING YOUR GOAL IN A NEGATIVE OR RESTRICTING TONE

The motivations for changing your life can start out negative. Once, I had a friend who just couldn't get serious about fitness and weight loss. Then one day at a backyard barbecue, he sat down on a plastic lawn chair, and it shattered under his weight. He was humiliated in front of his whole family, including his wife and young daughter. After that experience, he got serious. He didn't want a repeat of his public embarrassment. But while a negative event can be powerfully motivating, you should never express your goals in a negative or condescending way.

Remember, to be successful and feel fulfilled, you need to remain encouraged about the process. If you frame your goal as taking away or forbidding something, you'll feel like you're punishing yourself. "No drinking in 2024" feels very different from "I choose to be alcohol-free for one year!" The first statement sounds like a restriction, while the second feels like a powerful personal conviction. This should also be something you're excited about achieving. Keep your focus and energy on the positive impact it will have on your life and everything you will gain from the process of achieving this goal.

GOAL MISTAKE NO. 7: NOT CELEBRATING AND ACKNOWLEDGING THE SMALL WINS

Success doesn't usually show up as a big splash. It usually comes in small steps. Enjoying the process means celebrating tiny wins. I want you to play a game you can win. If your goal is to lose twenty pounds, and you lose one, you don't mourn that you still have nineteen to go. You high-five the shit out of everyone that the scale shows a lower number and that your work is paying off! Small steps—saving $50, paying down your credit card by $300, doing two more bench press reps—add up over time.

Take pleasure and joy in every step of progress, no matter how small. In all my time working with clients, I've found the following to be true:

Those who struggle to celebrate the small wins often never get the opportunity to celebrate the big wins.

Their negativity and discouragement make them give up before they even get close to the big wins. A great client success story illustrates this, and all it took was having her rip some shots every morning. OK, before you submit me to the authorities, let me explain. To this day, no matter their goal, I ask all my clients to drink more *water* because water leads to better energy and health, and better energy equals better days. So immediately after waking up, as they start their day, I have them drink sixteen ounces of water. Most people do this with no problem, but a former fitness client, Ashley, was having a hard time with it.

She would take one sip, look at the glass, get in her head about how she didn't think she could finish it, and eventually, she wouldn't even take a second sip. By day three, she would look at the filled glass, know she wouldn't be able to finish it, and not even take a single sip. This is a great example of the principle that says, "We like to play games we think we can win, and if we don't think we can win, we don't even want to play."

Finally, I said, "Ashley, do you have a shot glass?" She did. I said, "I want you to fill a shot glass full of water and put it in front of the coffee machine. Drink just that shot glass every morning." She thought the idea was ridiculous but agreed to humor me. When she woke up, she'd see the shot glass, a grin would come across her face, she'd rip the shot, and then she'd fill up her coffee. She told me it was easy, and I said, "Awesome. You're drinking two ounces of water. This is great. Next week, take two shots." Now she started taking two shots—four ounces of water before her coffee.

A few weeks later, she called me all excited and said, "Brett, guess what I did this morning! I drank all sixteen ounces of water before my coffee! Eight shots!" I laughed, but it was awesome. I'm also the only coach I know of who has his clients rip shots to start their day.

A shot glass of water was a game that Ashley felt she could win, and because of that, she was willing to play. It didn't have to be big; it had to be something that made her feel successful and something that made her want to play again tomorrow. That's the power of playing a game you think you can win. You set yourself up so if you do what you're supposed to do four days out of seven, you win the week. If you hit your daily reps, you win the day. If you get an extra thirty minutes of sleep, you win. You start "stacking wins," and over time, they stack up to make a big difference in your life.

Here's a simple formula to recap this chapter on how to set goals:

- Goal without a Deadline = **Wish**
- Goal + Deadline = **Target**
- Goal + Deadline + Consequence = **Commitment**
- Goal + Deadline + Consequence + Plan = **Intention**
- Goal + Deadline + Consequence + Plan + Deliberate Action = **Success**

Now this looks good to most. But success without fulfillment is not success at all. So what is the missing ingredient to this formula that most people overlook? (Refer back to common mistake No. 5.) It must be a goal that is personally meaningful to you. That makes all the difference. Add that in, and now we have a powerful formula:

- Personally Meaningful Goal + Deadline + Consequence + Plan + Deliberate Action = **Fulfillment**

Setting and pursuing goals should make you happy and pump you up. Accomplishing big goals will take time and hard work, so it's crucial to make sure you aren't wasting energy chasing down empty, unsatisfying goals. Instead, focus on goals that leave you feeling proud, accomplished, and fulfilled. That's the secret.

MOMENTUM BUILDERS

NOW: Review any current goal or think about goals you've been wanting to set. Have you made any of the common mistakes with choosing and setting your goals? If so, read the appropriate solution section and make the necessary changes.

TODAY: What is the "shot glass" version of your biggest goal? How can you play a smaller game that will let you rack up some wins toward your bigger goal? Decide what that is and have some fun taking small but meaningful steps toward success and fulfillment.

THE ABC METHOD—ACTION BUILDS CONFIDENCE

Back when I first started working for myself, I started making motivational apparel as a way to make some additional income, to have something to hand out to clients, and to help market my brand in town. I was always playing around with different words and phrases, and if it didn't work for apparel, it was still helpful for me to think through catchy, memorable one-liners and acronyms for my content and strategies—many of which appear in this book. My MOT-IVA-TED sweatshirts, with the word displayed in a three-by-three letter square, were easily my best sellers.

One day, while working on ideas and phrases related to confidence, I tried to think of a simple acronym. During one of my group coaching calls, in the middle of a passionate rant about taking action, I blurted out, "And that's why action builds confidence. Action builds confidence. It must go in that order." Someone in the chat typed, "Wow, Brett, that's such a simple method for confidence."

That was it. The ABC Method was born: Action Builds Confidence.

I shared it with my clients, and everybody loved it because it was catchy and easy to remember. Within a few days, everyone was quoting it back to me and telling me that whenever they felt stuck or felt fear or imposter syndrome creeping in, they remembered the ABC Method and just took immediate action. Because of that, they felt their confidence increasing with every action step they took. I've used it ever since.

But what does "Action Builds Confidence" mean? Everyone wants confidence, and they want it in advance so they can use it to face the uncomfortable decision or choice in front of them. The problem is that people seem to think they can will themselves to be confident—or even worse, fake it till you make it—and that's not how confidence works. Yes, there are some naturally confident people, but even they have had to put in reps. For most of us, confidence comes when we've already done something successfully multiple times—when we do what author and super-entrepreneur Alex Hormozi calls *stacking proof*.

Stacking proof is as simple as looking at recent history and saying, "Yeah, I've gone four straight months without using my credit card, so I know I can keep doing it," or "The last five times I've gone grocery shopping, I haven't bought any junk food, so I know I've got this." When you stack proof, you realize that because you've done the thing, you can keep doing it. That's where confidence comes from, not from some ephemeral part of your brain. This whole book is about doing the damn thing—not just talking about it, reading it, thinking about it, or dreaming about it but taking action first and letting action lead to more action.

That's the ABC Method.

CALLING BULLSHIT

We obsess over getting things right, especially in new situations. We become self-conscious and apologize for not being perfect. But contrary to popular wisdom, it only takes one success to fuel others. My wife and I love to play beach volleyball, and we work with a great coach. He could be drilling me on a new skill, and I could do it wrong the first twenty-five times—and then I get it right once. He'll say, "Stop. Think about that last rep. Close your eyes and put that one in your memory bank. Save that one." He wants me to file the one I got right in my memory and not worry about the other twenty-five because that one is proof that I got it right and that I can do it again. It takes practice and a growth mindset to allow yourself to celebrate the one good rep instead of the twenty-five incorrect ones. However, one success is all the evidence you need. Don't let anyone tell you otherwise.

REP ONE

One of the reasons I came up with the ABC Method was to counter the idea that you can just summon up confidence. That's bass-ackward. If you've never even tried something, your confidence that you can do it is probably going to be minimal at best. That's normal. We all doubt ourselves. It's kind of a law of human behavior, in fact.

WE ALWAYS DOUBT UNTIL AFTER THE FACT

Most of us don't really believe deep down that we can do something until after we've done it. It's why even though we know it can happen, we don't really believe that working out and eating right will help us lose weight until we look in the mirror after two months and go, "Holy shit, I'm thinner!" That's why ABC makes so much sense and is perfect for us mere mortals. It's a tool that works even if your first attempt at something is not 100 percent successful because action builds confidence in not one but *three* ways.

1. **It proves to you that you can do the thing and do it well.** You can finish the killer workout, complete your retirement plan, or show up on a first date with great energy.
2. **It proves to you that you can make mistakes and the world won't end.** I saw this all the time in my fitness coaching days. Men and women would be too self-conscious to come to the gym because they were out of shape or didn't know how to do yoga poses or burpees. Once they showed up and went through their first session or class, they saw that nobody cared how out of shape or awkward they were. In fact, most regular gym goers were positive and supportive because they had been there themselves once upon a time.
3. **It proves to you that you can take action, no matter the outcome.** For any of the single ladies, I call this "approaching McDreamy." Think about being in a bar or coffee shop, checking out some hot guy. If you have the nerve to go up and talk to him, you're a hero even if you get shot down. Just being able to do something scary is exhilarating, and it makes you more capable of doing it again. One of the top traits of all high performers is

overwhelming resilience. So it's good practice to get shot down every once in a while and prove that you can dust yourself off and try again. Of course, there's also the chance that you'll win!

You can think of confidence versus fear as something like the visual that follows with the following wording:

- **Before You Start = BIG FEAR, little confidence**
- **After Rep One = Fear shrinks, confidence grows**
- **After Many Reps = Little fear, BIG CONFIDENCE**

ABC means you don't have to fake it till you make it. In fact, here is exactly why faking it doesn't work: Confidence is found in repetition, preparation, and, most importantly, authenticity. When you're faking confidence, people read right through that—and you do too. You know you don't have that real confidence, and because you're attempting to fake it, you feel inauthentic.

When you feel inauthentic, you cannot also feel confident. The more you fake confidence, the more you emphasize that you don't have it.

The action doesn't even have to be that big to make a difference. Suppose you're walking into day one of a new job and are anxiously excited for the new challenge. Instead of faking it like you know everything, you decide to ask as many questions as you can. In doing so, you authentically acknowledge that you are beginning something new, while building authentic confidence with each question you find an answer to.

It's the same with hanging a new door for your backyard shed, investing in your first stock, or cooking a meal for your partner if you have no experience in the kitchen. After rep one you don't just gain confidence that you can repeat that action. You become a different person, a more capable person, in your own eyes. The ABC Method is the authentic antidote for impostor syndrome.

EMBRACE THE SUCK

Before I drop another acronym, allow me to address one of the most common issues that stops people from taking action and building confidence: the fear of being judged by others. Mega-bestselling author Brené Brown, in her TED Talk and her book *Daring Greatly*, calls this concept the FFT—fucking first time. There is no getting around the fact that the FFT is going to suck and be super uncomfortable. She talks about how as adults we retreat from trying certain new things because we don't want to experience the embarrassment of making mistakes or looking incompetent. Overcoming that fear is a matter of breaking the illusion that inaction and anonymity are better than taking a small risk—the risk of looking silly—for the potential of a big reward.

Here's an example. From time to time, I speak at events and in programs for prospective coaches eager to start their coaching careers. For a lot of them, that means building their brand on social media and consistently sharing content. But the idea of putting themselves out there on social media and sharing knowledge scares them because then the whole world can judge them. I might be in an online session with forty aspiring coaches, and I'll tell them that it's time to pull the trigger—to record video or write content telling people what they do. Many of them freeze because this is becoming real. Their friends follow them. Their former or current full-time employers follow them. They don't want to look stupid. They're terrified of being judged negatively. But here's what I've found:

The people who are judging are rarely the ones ahead of you.

Why would the people who are ahead of you bother judging? They don't need to, and they don't have the time. In my experience successful people are the first to lend a helping hand and offer constructive criticism to newbies because they know and respect how hard it is to make the climb. It's never one founder or business owner judging another. It's the ones who can't make the climb who talk smack and criticize, usually because they're too scared to try themselves. So they focus their time and attention on throwing shade at others who take the risks and try new things. But if those people don't have the courage or confidence to step into the arena themselves, why does their opinion matter?

It doesn't. So quit stopping yourself because you fear judgment.

Here's how I proved this to my coaching mentees. I had everybody take out their phones, open Instagram, and record a thirty-second video pitching their coaching program. It didn't have to be polished or perfect; I just wanted them to each get a practice rep under their belt. But I wanted them to get excited. I wanted them to stop overthinking and *just do it*! So they all hit Mute and recorded their videos while we were on the call, and a few minutes later, they all came back on.

Then the tough love side of my coaching showed up. I said, "Good. Now I want everyone to post it right now. Don't think about it. Don't edit it. Don't record it again. Just put it up." Everybody went pale. The vibe was, "Oh my God, I can't believe he's making me do this." But they all posted their videos. That is the essence of uncomfort. While they may have hated me in the moment, they all understood this was necessary to conquer the FFT together as a group.

On our next call, I asked, "Hey, did anybody die after posting that video? Is everybody still breathing? Did anyone get tons of hate? Do you all still hate me?" Of course, everybody was fine, and many even received encouraging messages from their friends, family, and other followers. That was rep one for many of them. It was a big deal, and learning that they could do it was a huge step toward achieving their career goals. Just like many birds would never know they had the ability to fly if mom didn't push them out of the nest and force them to find out. It's seductive to stay in that unknown space, and you can do that, be safe, and not risk anything. Or you can lean into uncomfort, take a little risk, and do something where the potential payoff could change your life.

UNCOMFORTABLE TRUTH NO. 8

Confidence is attractive. Arrogance is not.

Having confidence is fantastic. It's a critical part of your journey to your long-term vision. But when confidence crosses over into arrogance, it becomes a curse. Arrogance is the belief that your ability to do some things better than most people makes you superior to them as a person—smarter, more virtuous, more worthwhile. That's ugly. The best and most respected CEOs and founders are the ones who exude extreme confidence to their teams and to the world yet still remember how it felt to be the little guy making the climb. As you gain confidence, remember to keep your humility. It's easy. Just think about how much you sucked when you started doing whatever you do.

ACTION IS RELATIVE

Every time you take action in an area where you lack confidence, it's like putting a vote of confidence in your mental and emotional piggy bank. Every time you act, it becomes easier to do it again. The action and your goal become less remote and more familiar. That's why action builds confidence. There is magic in repetition and familiarity.

One thing to remember as you're facing an action that makes you nervous: a small action for someone else might be a huge step for you. *The size of any action is relative.* I've been speaking now for years, and I'm comfortable putting myself out there even if some people in the audience don't fully resonate with my style. That doesn't bother me, but it might crush someone who walked to the podium for the first time with relatively little experience.

So don't let other people's actions dictate what your next action should be. If you've never taken a yoga class before, going to your first class may feel like climbing a mountain. If you've never started a small business, filing your first LLC paperwork might be as stressful and tiring as running a 10K. There's no absolute scale that determines the value of any action. If it gives you more confidence, it's worthwhile. Period.

However, I will say that, generally speaking:

- **Small action = small confidence boost**
- **Large action = large confidence boost**

Let me reiterate that there's *nothing* wrong with a small confidence boost. Sometimes, it's all you need, and some days, it's all you can manage to prevent a *zero day*. But in general, the amount of confidence you get from your action correlates with the size of the action. Singing in front of your drunk friends at karaoke night might give you a little hit of confidence that you can sing in front of people, but singing in the community variety show in front of three hundred audience members, most of whom don't know you, is like gulping down a gallon of confidence, even if your knees are shaking.

This is where the mantra "embrace the suck" comes into play. The phrase comes from the US military, and it means that since you can't avoid the current miserable situation, you might as well lean into it and make it work for you. If your *rep one* is going to make your palms sweat and your heart pound but reaching your goals means doing it anyway, then embrace the suck—the uncomfort—get it done, and high-five the crap out of everyone after you do.

My advice: *Start small.* Taking action of any size demystifies your goal. You walk through the door and join the club of people who can "do it." That's true even if your first actions are modest. Just remember to escalate your actions as you become more confident. First, file the LLC. Then hire someone to design your website. Then sign a lease on a storefront. Next, give your notice at your job. That's escalating. Each action is bigger, riskier, and scarier than the last, but with each one, you'll become more confident that you can handle the next one.

THE ABC PROCESS

1. **Set your goal.** Know the endgame. It always comes back to knowing where you're heading. Be sure you don't make any of the seven goal-setting mistakes.
2. **Figure out the steps.** What's your plan? What do you have to do, in sequence, to be where you want to be? Don't skip any steps, and if you're more apt to stay consistent with smaller actions, break any bigger steps down into multiple smaller ones.
3. **Take the first action.** This is where that FFT feeling will likely come into play and where anxiety lives. You can handle it. Embrace the suck, and get through your first rep as quickly as you can so you can start shrinking the fear and growing your confidence.
4. **Learn from the experience.** You're going to pick up knowledge from taking action and more lessons from failure and losing than you will from success. Use it all to fuel each next rep.
5. **Take inventory.** How do you feel? Did you survive mistakes and embarrassment? Are you more confident about the next step? Is it time for a bigger action, or should you dial back to a smaller step and find a game you know you can win?
6. **Repeat.** Every time you notice a lack of confidence, it's a reminder that you haven't taken enough action in this area. Go back to step one and begin taking the necessary action required to build your confidence.

MOMENTUM BUILDERS

NOW: Take one small action that serves your goal and will immediately boost your confidence. It doesn't matter what it is: signing up for a gym membership, asking someone to be your mentor, booking a flight to the place you think you might want to relocate. Close this book and give the ABC Method your first test drive.

TODAY: List two other areas of your life where you would benefit from an increase in confidence. Next to each one, write down one small, immediate action you can take before the end of the day. Yes, these first steps will take courage, but now you know that confidence only comes *after* the action. Go make it happen.

MOMENTUM KICKS MOTIVATION'S ASS

Plenty of folks think the key to reaching goals is motivation. Here's why that's wrong. You might be motivated to do something and think that motivation will last all year. But motivation is like a battery; it can power you up but will eventually run out of juice. You won't even notice your motivation draining until one day you go to tap into that energy and realize your motivation is dead. By the time you find new motivation, a month has passed.

Motivation is not a reliable way to keep yourself on course and working consistently toward your goals. The first reason is that *all motivation is temporary.* Let's say you have a dentist appointment coming up, and you want a good checkup. So two weeks before your appointment, you start flossing every night and brushing meticulously. While you don't exactly fool your dentist, you also find you don't have any cavities. You high-five your dentist, leave the clinic feeling great . . . and immediately abandon your new extensive flossing routine. Why? Because your dental checkup is over. Now you reward yourself and begin to slack off. Your motivation and your urgency are gone. This is why most people conclude their annual Dry January spells by popping open a beer or pouring a glass of wine. Proof that they were only committed to the time frame of the challenge, not the actual process of the change.

The second reason motivation doesn't work very well is that it's reward-based. We think our goals will motivate us, and they can, but only for a short time. Humans are bad at thinking long term. We're motivated by short-term goals: looking hot at our high school reunion, saving enough money to buy a Tesla, getting out of a crappy job. Once we reach those goals—or once it becomes clear that we *won't* reach them—we tend to backslide. Long-term motivation is about rewards, from the desire to get pleasure or avoid pain. But you're moving toward uncomfort, toward pain, and it's hard to motivate yourself to do that. When you're beginning a program of change, you can't depend on motivation to show up consistently because the reward isn't there yet.

CALLING BULLSHIT

Rewards are not as motivating as you think they are. One of the reasons motivation doesn't work is because positive motivations lack teeth. "I want to be healthy and live a long time for my kids" just doesn't have the same punch as "I'm tired of being embarrassed by my kids always joking that 'Daddy must be pregnant.' That's not the example I want to set for them, and that's not how I want them to remember me." So just maybe, quit worrying about your motivations being nice and politically correct and grab the ones that spark your real emotion and desire. The reality is, pain and consequences generate more motivation than pleasure.

THE WORST COMEBACK OF ALL TIME

But plenty of books talk about motivation, and that is far from the takeaway I want you to walk away with, so let's leave it there. I'm not a fan of relying on motivation to get you where you want to be, and you shouldn't be either. What I am a big fan of is *momentum*, the tendency of a body in motion to stay in motion. Here's a fantastic example of what momentum can do (and because I'm a born and raised Yankee fan, this story is painful for me to relive, but I do it all for you).

In October 2004, the Boston Red Sox were playing the New York Yankees in the American League Championship Series to see which team would go to the World Series. The Yankees had humiliated the Red Sox in the postseason in recent years, and they were up three games to none in the 2004 series. No team had ever come back from being down three to none. All they had to do was win one more game, and the series was over. It was the bottom of the ninth inning with the Red Sox at bat, and the Yankees led 4–3 with two out. The speedy Dave Roberts was on first base, but just about everyone in Red Sox Nation had given up hope, and us Yankee fans were beginning to celebrate another trip to the World Series. Then Roberts, with an entire stadium of people expecting him to try to steal, stole second base, the biggest steal in Boston history. Two pitches later, the hitter lined a single up the middle to tie the game, 4–4. The Red Sox wound up winning that game 6–4 in a twelve-inning thriller.

Big deal, right? Nothing much had changed. It was only one game. Sure, the Yankees had blown a late lead, but otherwise, the players were the same. The talent level was the same. The history was the same. The pressure was all on the Sox. But somehow, momentum had shifted. Even if just by a little. I remember watching the next three games with my high school buddies. The following night, when the Red Sox won their second game, Game 5, we all had this strange feeling like we had become the underdog, even though we were still ahead in the series. It made no sense, but we just felt the energy change. The momentum had shifted, and everybody knew it. We didn't know how we knew it, but it was like the

Sox suddenly had the wind at their backs. It wasn't that they became more motivated. They had created unstoppable momentum. Of course, the Red Sox went on to stage the biggest postseason comeback in Major League history and win that series 4–3.

Momentum is a force to be reckoned with. It kicks motivation's ass as a way to keep you moving toward your milestones and your long-term vision. There are a bunch of reasons why.

- **Momentum is largely in your control.** Sure, the momentum shift for the Red Sox seemed to come out of nowhere, but it really started with Dave Roberts's stolen base. One small act started the boulder rolling down the hill. That's all it takes. One small move, one small choice. All you have to do is act. Motivation, on the other hand, can become irrelevant at any time.
- **You don't need to find it; you create it.** Momentum comes when you get up, get moving, and do the damn thing. That's why Nike chose "Just do it" as their slogan. Probably because "just think about it" or "just wait until you feel like it" don't have the same punch.
- **Momentum builds on itself.** If you win early, you can "draft" off your previous wins on days when you don't feel like showing up. Once you get past a certain point in a workout program or a certain number in your savings account, you don't want to give back the progress you've made, so you persist. The snowball gets bigger and bigger with each roll down the mountain.

The power of momentum comes from its simplicity. You don't need a higher purpose. You don't need anything but forward motion. Carrying out your daily plan becomes just that thing you do, regardless of how you feel. That's when you rack up wins—when taking action and making good choices become automatic.

UNCOMFORTABLE TRUTH NO. 9

Not all movement is momentum.

Momentum can be powerful, but only when you're headed in the right direction. If you don't take the time to clearly establish your destination and set precise targets for yourself, you might find yourself expending effort without progressing. This is because not all movement equals momentum and why being busy doesn't always mean you're making progress. Consider this: taking six random steps is far less effective than taking two steps in the direction of your desired destination. Only focused momentum creates tangible progress. It amplifies the impact of your efforts, transforming sporadic actions into a journey toward success. So get moving, but make sure you're moving intentionally and in the direction you want to go.

NBD

Notice a minute ago that I said momentum is what *keeps* you moving? What about getting you moving from a standing position, which most would argue is 95% of the battle? What about getting you out of bed, off the couch, or out of the house? What about *starting* momentum? That's about your NBD, your Next Best Decision.

Let's assume that because you're reading this book, you haven't yet pressed PLAY on your grand plan for changing your life. Cool. Starting from nothing is great because you don't have to undo any mistakes. So what's going to get you moving from where you are right now? Your

NBD—your next best decision. As you sit there, at this moment, reading these words, stop and think, "What could I do next that would represent immediate progress toward my goal, no matter how small?"

Could you get up and drink a glass of water? Eat some fruit? Use your online banking app to transfer $500 into your IRA? Call your business partner to set up a meeting for this afternoon? Reactivate your gym membership?

Did you think of something? Your next best decision is something you can decide on and do right now. As in, this moment. Any longer than that and it's not actually your *next* best decision. Decide quick, act quick, like shot-glass quick. Put the book down and do it. Right now. I'll wait.

[Brett hums *Jeopardy!* theme song . . .]

Welcome back. See how easy that was? No, that one act didn't change your life, but it was the first step in building momentum. Now within the next hour, make another next best decision. Then another, and another, and another. When you can pile up three to seven consecutive days of doing things that make a small but meaningful difference in your situation—the core actions that are in your contract—that's when you will start to believe, "I can do this!" The momentum builders at the end of each chapter are designed to help you make your *next best decision*.

Once you get to that point, you're ready to make the next jump: consistently accomplishing the *most important* part of your plan. That could be eating vegan, seeing a therapist, building your pitch deck, or whatever moves the needle most. The best way to build significant momentum is to start and finish the most important part of your plan as consistently as possible. When you do that, you quickly become *invested*. You won't want to deviate and lose momentum.

For example, suppose you've worked out six days a week for the last three weeks, and you're tempted to take three days off to go to Vegas. When momentum is at your back, you're more likely to say "I'm not going to blow the last three weeks by slacking off. I've worked too hard. I'll go to Vegas, but I'm hitting the hotel gym before I play a hand of blackjack." And that's exactly what you do. *Maintaining your momentum has become more important than reverting to old habits.*

Momentum is like a wave. Each tiny bit of momentum is like a breeze blowing across the ocean and creating a tiny wave of momentum. The more you do, the higher and higher the wave gets. It might start small, but it can turn into a tsunami. When you look at people who are crushing life, who are fit and wealthy and have incredible success, you're looking at people who have been taking consistent action for years and have a tsunami of momentum behind them. You might think, "They're so disciplined." Well, yes and no. They just showed up every day. If you do something five days a week for a year, you'll have a tsunami of momentum pushing you forward. It's not easy to stop that. When you have that much momentum, it's easier to feel disciplined. It's as hard to stop good habits as it is to start new habits.

NO, THE OTHER NBD

But what happens when momentum stalls? What happens when you've been going great for six months, and then you get sick or a crisis happens at work, causing your momentum to drain down to nothing? That's a terrible feeling because you worked so hard to build up that momentum, but things aren't hopeless. NBD has another meaning besides "next best decision," and they pair perfectly. It also means "no big deal."

If your momentum dries up and you feel dead in the water, it's no big deal. Just make your next best decision. You've built up a tsunami once; you can do it again. Just take action in the moment—no delays. My old football coach, Coach Vogt, used to say, "We're one play away. Who's going to make the game-altering play where we steal all the momentum back?" What's the next action that will get you moving in the right direction again? If you doubt that it's possible to get back on track with a single action, think about the 2004 Red Sox. One steal of second base created a wave, and finding a way to win Game 4 created a tsunami. It changed everything. What's your "steal of second" that almost feels too small to get the wheel turning?

As you start to gain momentum, you'll know it. It's palpable. You can feel the energy. You'll become more confident as you consistently stick to your routine, and other people might even comment on your new, more badass posture, speech, and demeanor. Another signal of rising momentum is that setbacks become bumps in the road, not insurmountable obstacles. What used to stop you now barely slows you down. You learn how to bounce back from setbacks, adapt, and continue.

You'll probably find yourself drawn to positive influences and resources that align with your goals—books, speakers, online content, seminars, and other sources of inspiration. This is because once you build up some momentum, you feel like you're in the club. You're off the sidelines and onto the field. You finally belong with the achievers, not with the wannabes with their noses pressed up against the glass, watching other people live the great life.

FIFTY VERSUS FIFTY-ONE

Speaker and author Judith M. Bardwick once wrote, "Motivation is highest when the probability of success is fifty percent. We don't get involved if the task is too easy or too hard."* This brings us back to limiting beliefs, and I'd argue that for most of us, fifty isn't enough. But if you can get yourself to *fifty-one*, that's where the game changes. If you believe your odds of winning are just slightly higher than not, that becomes a game

* Bardwick, Judith M. *Danger in the Comfort Zone : From Boardroom to Mailroom–How to Break the Entitlement Habit That's Killing American Business*. 1995. Amacom.

you think you can win, and that's a game you'll be willing to play, even if it's hard.

Sometimes, that extra 1 percent comes from creating a little momentum. Once you see results, motivation and belief become easier. It's easier to keep working out once you see your pants fitting better, and it's easier to save money when you see your bank balance top $100,000. Remember, we only really believe something is possible after the fact.

That's why it's so important to keep your head down, show up, and not worry about immediate results. The results will be there, but if you rely on results for motivation, you could wind up in trouble because results will never come fast enough to satisfy your expectations. As hard as you might try, you might not see massive changes on your first, second, or even third attempt to reach your goal. The pressure to see results quickly can lead to burnout and unfair expectations, which is why it's important to remember that growth requires patience, resilience, and self-compassion.

While we'd all like to stay on the horse and ride into the sunset on our first try, the truth is that getting back on the horse after we fall off is what separates the winners from the losers. Try resolving to not look at the scale for thirty days or at the value of your stock portfolio for one quarter. Just show up, do what you're supposed to do, and don't worry about the results. They'll be there.

MOMENTUM BUILDERS

NOW: Make another next best decision right now. Put down the book and go do it, no matter how small it is. Again, if this really is your *next* best decision, this should, at max, take you a minute or two.

TODAY: Make your "no big deal" plan. This is the exact plan and steps you will put into action to get moving again if and when you lose your momentum. I hope it won't be necessary, but hope is not a strategy. It's better to have a solid plan B that you're confident in, and that will get momentum back on your side.

CHAPTER 10

NEVER MISS A MONDAY

For years, I hated Mondays. I proudly waved the *I hate Monday* flag. I couldn't even enjoy a Sunday without the anxiety of a looming Monday and the upcoming week creeping in to steal my Sunday peace and joy. That's what some people call the "Sunday Scaries," the dread that hits on Sunday when you know the workweek is just around the corner. Freedom is over, and we're supposed to hate going back to our obligations. For some it's not just the week ahead but also the realization that occurs on Sundays about where our life is—or, more importantly, where our life isn't and what we're not doing to change it. That causes some real anxiety.

That was me for a long time. Then, looking for a major life makeover, I started going to conferences and studying high performers, business owners, and motivational speakers. I had one of those moments that stops you in your tracks. I realized, "Wait a minute, these people don't hate Mondays. They love Mondays. Monday's actually their best day." It was a light bulb moment. Everybody else hated Mondays, but these successful people loved them. What was the difference?

After a while I saw the pattern. They had a plan. They had purpose. They were headed in a clear direction. *And they took both ownership and control of their Mondays.* They woke up on Monday excited about their specific plan to dominate rather than feeling like they were just going to get thrown back into the machine again.

I decided I would do whatever it took to become someone who loved Mondays. I made sure that I got up early on Mondays. At the gym, I started to work my favorite muscle groups on Monday (back and shoulders, if you're wondering). I made sure that the first couple of hours of my Monday were always about personal growth. I would work out, watch a motivational video, and eat a healthy breakfast all before my workday even started. After a few weeks of dominating my Monday mornings like this, another light bulb went off when I saw the correlation. When I had a good Monday, I was more likely to have a good Tuesday. When I had a good Monday *and* Tuesday, I was more likely to have a good Wednesday. You can see where I'm going with this.

That's where my motto, "Never Miss a Monday," came from. While I can't exactly take full credit for that (it's all over the internet), I take a ton of pride in how many people never miss a Monday because of how long I've been sharing and posting about it. It's been more than thirteen years since I first championed the "Never Miss a Monday" motto, and I still get tagged on social media in people's #NMAM posts. I freakin' love it. It works. Nobody who has ever worked with me or been in my sphere of influence for any amount of time would ever miss a Monday workout.

Over time NMAM has evolved into much more than just not missing a workout. It grew into "Never miss the opportunity to start the week in complete control of everything that's important to you." If your marriage is important to you, NMAM to give your partner a huge hug and kiss to start the day and let them know how much they mean to you. If changing your relationship with money is important to you, NMAM to open your bank statements and review your money plan for the week. Never Miss a Monday is a weekly launchpoint and checkpoint and reminder that each week we get a blank slate of opportunities to take advantage of. If last week sucked, never miss a Monday. If last week was amazing, never miss a Monday. You cannot allow week after week to slip by without being in control.

In an attempt to connect the high-performance dots even further, I started working backward. You can't have a good week without having a good Monday, and you can't have a good day without having a good morning. Logically, you can't have a good morning without a good night's sleep, and you can't have a good night's sleep unless you really start the whole process on Sunday. So you need a good Sunday to have a good Monday.

Still with me? Good!

Eventually, this will lead us to my Sunday planning process, "the Sunday Setup," but right now I want to talk about having a plan. Because whether it's Monday or Thursday, planning is everything. Dwight D. Eisenhower said, "Plans are nothing; planning is everything," and Ike was right. A plan is a list on a piece of paper; planning is actively mapping out and taking control of your time.

Planning is the only way you get to that hyperproductive Monday where you're getting so much done but don't feel tired because being focused and moving the needle is exhilarating. Those Mondays lead to better Tuesdays, which lead to you winning your week, then your month, and then your year. Again, simple but not easy. Mondays are contagious, for better or worse. If your Monday currently sucks, you're not only battling uphill from the starting line; you're also forcing yourself to play the game of life at a self-imposed disadvantage.

If you want your Mondays to be better, you need two things: a major makeover in energy and attitude, and a plan, so let's talk about making one.

CALLING BULLSHIT

A study published in the journal *Psychological Science* found that Monday is the most productive day for embarking on self-improvement programs or trying new things.* Nobody is 100 percent sure why, but they think it's because on Monday we have the sense of "starting over," like we do on New Year's Day. But you know what this study didn't show? How many of those people quit those programs by the end of the week? Yes, of course, I think adopting the "Never Miss a Monday" mentality will be incredibly valuable and helpful for you. However, by no means am I encouraging you to *wait* to start on Monday. If you don't learn to start things on random Wednesdays, Fridays, or any other day and stop waiting to generate momentum, you are always going to struggle with consistency. Momentum can't afford to wait until Monday or the beginning of a new month. Dominate Monday, but don't be like all the other people who allow six days to go by before they restart again on Monday. Restart *immediately*, and be better than the average crowd that can only start things on a Monday.

PLAYING OFFENSE

Setting big goals sounds really cool to people, and it gets people fired up, but none of that really matters unless you start playing offense. You take inventory, start playing offense, and then determine the big vision you want to aim for. Most people do the opposite. They play defense. They allow factors that are out of their control—events at work, family stuff, the weather—to rearrange their priorities and determine what they can accomplish. You'll never achieve anything if you're continually playing defense because you'll inevitably become delayed and distracted by everything and anyone looking to grab at your time.

* Dai, H., K. L. Milkman, and J. Riis. "Put Your Imperfections Behind You: Temporal Landmarks Spur Goal Initiation When They Signal New Beginnings." *Psychological Science* 26, no. 12 (2015), 1927-1936. https://doi.org/10.1177/0956797615605818.

Remember at the start of the book, when I talked about demoting myself in my fitness job so I'd have more time to pursue my dream of starting my own business? That was a massive step that took me from defense to finally playing offense. Playing offense means having a plan that gives you control over everything that you can control. In your plan you identify your most common excuses for not working out or not saving money so you can find ways to avoid getting tripped up by them. You set an aggressive but realistic schedule so you can make the most of your time. You lay out the things you need to do to keep your environment optimal for reaching your goals—for example, making a weekly grocery delivery order so you always have healthy food on hand. Having a plan means leaving nothing to chance. It means you no longer just have a target or a commitment, but an intention. It means *anticipating* the traps and obstacles that are most likely to keep you from doing what you need to do and avoiding them in advance. Basically, having a plan means being Batman—knowing where the pitfalls will be before they even show up. That's how you stay ahead and keep winning.

I should probably explain the difference between *high performers* and *inconsistent high performers*. I've met plenty of people who appeared impressive and successful who couldn't begin to tell me their process for planning out their week, and it's shocking to me that they can do what they do. Most of the time, while successful on paper, these people are overwhelmed, are overworked, and have zero control over their time. Is that your definition of success? That's not what I want my life to look like, and you're probably the same way. People like that usually have extraordinary talent but are far from living a high-performance life. If we don't have otherworldly talent, we have to plan and execute with precision. If we do, we can often outperform the people who are talented but undisciplined!

Many people are *inconsistent high performers*. They have skills and potential, but they want to become the type of people who follow through consistently, keep their commitments, and have the grit to keep going when things get tough. They know they can't rely exclusively on their talent and skills. They're desperate to become more organized, improve their prioritization, and take back control of their time. Discipline is a developed trait. It's something you can improve, and it becomes easier when you're clear on your purpose and vision. When you're clear on what you want, it's easier to stay on target and on task.

This is where many people get discouraged because they struggle to articulate where they want to be in two, five, or ten years. If that's you, this next part is going to blow your mind. Because believe it or not, it also works if you're clear on what you *don't* want.

One client of mine—a successful CFO, a great father, and a great husband—had plenty of goals but was also struggling to articulate out his long-term plan. He had a hard time looking down the road and was getting down on himself for not knowing where he wanted to be in five years. Finally, I tried a different strategy. I told him that he didn't need to know what he wanted his life to look like—because if he could get super clear on what he *didn't* want life to be like in five years, that was just as helpful to us. This allowed us to set up his guardrails.

His eyes got big, and it was like a new gust of wind hit his sails. He knew he didn't want to be overweight or less strong, so we put a plan together to keep him fit and in shape to avoid developing a dad bod. He didn't mind more responsibility at work but didn't want to be so busy that he couldn't coach his kids' baseball and soccer teams as they got older. So we made sure he was working toward a work schedule that would allow him flexibility in the evenings. He didn't want his wife to feel unappreciated, so I helped him plan four trips a year for just the two of them. That became his compass, his purpose. He was getting clear, not just on where he wanted to be but who he wanted to be. This made it easier for him to keep taking action and remaining disciplined with decisions that keep him firmly within his guardrails and heading toward a destination that he would be excited about. Why do some people have the drive and determination to get what they want, while others struggle to get started? Here's the secret. It's easy to have drive and determination when you know where you want to go. It's easier to get what you want when you know what *it* is. So before you start building your plan, ask yourself what you're planning toward. What's your vision of who you want to become or not become? Either one's fine as long as you're passionate about it and dedicated to playing offense. This is about harnessing strong emotions to help stay on track. Now let's plan.

TURNING HOPE INTO A STRATEGY

A good plan is like a software algorithm. Once you set it in motion, it runs and automates everything. You don't need willpower. You just follow the plan and check the boxes. For years I was a victim of my list of all the things I hoped to do. Unfortunately, hope is not a strategy, so it never got me very far. Then I decided to flip that thought on its head and call my strategy HOPE: **Have a Clear Target, Organize, Prioritize,** and **Execute.** This is the planning system I use for myself, and I began to teach it to my clients. I built it around a seven-day week, from Monday to Sunday. Now hope can actually be a strategy.

That's why Mondays are critical. I'm all about playing a game you can win, and a week is a manageable amount of time. Start with a Monday you can crush, all the way to your next Sunday Setup, which gets you ready for the following week. (Much more on the Sunday Setup in a bit.)

UNCOMFORTABLE TRUTH NO. 10

Not all things on your to-do list are weighted equally. There are always going to be one or two things in your day's plan that if you don't do them, the day feels like a failure. Back when I was in the fitness industry, I could sell five gym memberships, train eight great clients, and eat a great lunch, but if I missed my own workout, I still felt like I was unproductive that day. I had done everything for everybody else, but I couldn't do the one thing that I was promoting. I felt like a fraud. Yes, you should prioritize the things that serve your vision, but don't forget about the thing that means more to you than anything else, whether that's meditating or having dinner with your family.

HAVE A CLEAR TARGET

What are you trying to accomplish? When you lay out your plan, first, set your rules. For example, let's say your perfect wellness day has five daily targets—exercise, drink one hundred ounces of water, sleep for eight hours, meditate, and so on. How many of those do you have to complete to "win the day"? Four, or 80 percent? Cool. So four is a win. Now how many days do you have to win in order to win your week? Seven days is setting the bar awfully high and feeds the perfectionist in us, so is five doable? Yeah, probably. That's 71 percent. So now if you're able to complete four out of five items per day, five days a week, you win the week! Before you know it, you've won the month.

(Yes, I am well aware that 71 percent would be a C- if we were in school, but 71 percent of a plan is better than 100 percent of nothing. You can always raise your standard as you go, but that won't matter if you never get started.)

On your computer or phone (use any medium you can take with you so your plan goes where you go), create a list that accounts for the following:

- Your entire week, Monday to Sunday
- Your daily schedule for activities such as exercise, grocery shopping, self-care, reading, meditation, family time, side hustles, sleep preparation, or therapy sessions.

Great start. But an effective target is more than a to-do list. You should also do an honest accounting of the temptations, bad habits, or compulsions that tend to make you slack off or quit. That way, you can plan to circumvent them. A simple example would be, "Donate, give away, or throw out any junk food that I don't want to be tempted by on Sunday night," if your goal is weight loss. But let's say you're trying to repair your relationship with your spouse, and one of your bad habits is obsessively watching TV after work. One of your preventive to-dos could be, "Lock away the remote control on Sunday unless I go for a long walk with my spouse." You're getting rid of temptation so you can focus your attention on your significant other. Proactively remove all opportunities to get sidetracked.

Include consequences in your plan to help prevent "I'll do better tomorrow" rationalizations. Write out, specifically, what will happen if you don't do your workout or if you overspend that day. Do you have to clean the house while your roommates watch TV? Do you have to put five dollars in the "Slacker Jar"? I'd love to tell you that rewards are all you need, but for many people, consequences are a lot more effective than rewards at holding them accountable. Figure out what holds you accountable and leverage it to your advantage.

One of the biggest mistakes I see people make in planning is having a great plan to start but a shitty plan to *finish*. A plan that gets you moving but doesn't get you to the end of the week is only 50 percent helpful. It's important to account for the reality that as the week goes on, we get tired. We get lazy. We rationalize and perhaps get less sleep. We make excuses, and we tend to bail. Because of that, a good plan should become *stricter* and more specific as you get into Friday, Saturday, and Sunday. You want to go out with friends on Saturday night? Okay, but did you hit your workouts for the week, or do you need Sunday morning to hit your target of five days? You want to buy those $200 concert tickets for Sunday? That means not eating lunch out all week prior. You bring food from home. See what I mean?

For those of you thinking the consequence idea is too harsh, I challenge you. That voice is your limiting beliefs desperate to keep you in comfort and stuck in Excuseville. You're not being harsh; you're finally empowering yourself by no longer letting yourself off the hook every time you don't want to follow through. Think back to all the rewards you promised yourself in the past. Didn't work as well as you thought they would, did they? Pain is a greater motivator than pleasure, so lean in.

Finally, manage your expectations. Include in your plan how hard you think some things will be and what you think you can realistically do. Whether you're talking about reps in the gym, dollars saved, or KPIs hit at work, set benchmarks that push you but don't require you to be superhuman. Change is hard; allow for that.

ORGANIZE

Organizing is about removing friction from your routine and getting rid of any extra complexity, effort, or steps that might tempt you to throw up your hands and say, "Forget it. I'll do it tomorrow." What can you clear off your plate that doesn't serve your long-term vision? What can you delegate? Part of this is about making sure you have everything in place to carry out your plan: equipment, trainers, software tools, food, whatever. Of course, it's also about organizing your time. One of my favorite techniques for this is to break the day into four quarters, like a football game.

- Quarter 1: Everything you do from the moment you wake up until you begin work.
- Quarter 2: The first half of your workday.
- Quarter 3: The last half of your workday.
- Quarter 4: Everything after work until bed.

Then focus on winning one quarter at a time. The same applies to winning in sport as it does your day. Never assume that a bad quarter equals a bad game. Is it easier to win the game when you've dominated the first quarter? Sure. However, lots of teams come back to win games in the fourth quarter. If you mess up and completely bomb a quarter, make your NBD. Attack the next quarter as your chance to right the ship. Every day is a new chance to play the game and get it right. There are many different ways to win. Don't dwell on what you got wrong because it's not like you can go back and change it. Learn and move on. Winners focus on winning; losers focus on not losing.

PRIORITIZE

It's also important to use your plan to determine the right sequence of activities in your day and to allocate the right amount of time for the most important actions. Sequencing usually comes down to getting essentials out of the way early—working out, drinking water, eating a good breakfast, meditating, and so on. You can do the same thing with the end of your day, focusing on things such as reading, getting workout gear together for the next morning, setting your alarm, and going through your bedtime routine.

In between, you'll want to allocate time to the things that have the greatest impact on your big vision. I call these *needle moving activities*. For instance, if your big vision is a change in your career, then activities related to finding potential job opportunities that better align with your passion and purpose might be your number one priority Monday through Friday. You'll spend dedicated time updating your résumé, finding open positions that you are qualified for, seeking out referrals, and so on. If your vision is about starting your own company, you'll want to schedule things such as market research, hiring, working on your business plan, etc.

This is a great time to make use of calendaring and scheduling software, whether it's Google Calendar or an app such as Todoist, OneNote, or My Daily Planner. Set alarms and reminders and work through all your items, and you'll be amazed at how the time flies. Many coaches preach that how you do something is how you do everything. I couldn't disagree more. Because you could clean and reorganize your office better than you've ever done before, but if you were supposed to be spending that time replying to client emails and coming up with your Q2 business plan, you're still procrastinating. Watch out for sneaky traps like this. They're exactly why you might look back on a day feeling like you were busy and completed a lot of tasks but still didn't move the needle. Just like we established that not all movement is momentum, not all execution is productive. Which is why you need to prioritize and protect your time. Contrary to popular advice, how you do something is not nearly as important as *what* you do.

EXECUTE

Finally, execute your plan. Like I said, high performers generally are decent at execution, mostly because they look at it as removing, not adding. Execution is about simplifying your path to being and doing better. Is there anything you can make automatic?

Can you schedule an Uber to show up every morning at your house to take you to the gym? Can you set up autotransfer to contribute money to your 401(k) every month? Can you hire a housecleaning service so you have more time to work on your physical and mental health? Can you have your week's groceries delivered every week with the same healthy foods from the previous week? Execution can be as simple as putting your workout shoes and glass of water right next to your alarm clock before you go to bed so they're the first things you see the next morning.

Also, go through your daily schedule and clear away the "time vampires" that drain little bits of your time that add up to hours. Use a bill-paying service so you don't waste time writing checks. Subscribe to Blue Apron to have your meals delivered and ready to cook. Put your supplements on auto-delivery. If you find it impossible to stop binge-watching certain TV shows, cancel the streaming service that carries them. Quit the willpower fairy tale. Change is hard already; don't make it harder. Clear your path as much as possible of anything that pulls you away from your goal. As you develop new habits and sharpen your discipline, you can always add some of those guilty pleasures back—as long as you do it *carefully* and make sure they fit your HOPE strategy.

MOMENTUM BUILDERS

NOW: Break your current day into four quarters and ask yourself what you need to do to win each quarter you have left in your day. If you're at the end of your day, plan out exactly what you need to do tomorrow to win your first quarter.

TODAY: I've already mentioned that not all execution is productive. Where is one area you've been spending time and energy executing that is not moving the needle for you? Now choose whether you will eliminate, delegate, or at the very least automate this task to free up more of your time for things that will move the needle.

YOU'RE ONE OR TWO BIG DECISIONS AWAY FROM WINNING CONSISTENTLY

This idea came from the first high-performance conference I attended. Some of the speakers talked about how, if you came back to the same conference next year, you could be a completely different person, but only if you went back home and took action. That challenged my limiting beliefs. Could I really be a different person one year from now? That made me think, "Maybe I'm not as far away as I think. Maybe I'm closer than I thought."

But I knew the change I made couldn't be a small one. The ripple effect of a choice is like the difference between throwing a pebble into a pond and throwing in a boulder. I knew I needed the boulder. I had tried pebbles before, and playing it safe just never worked. Only a boulder, a big change, can cause enough downstream changes that it changes everything. So I demoted myself as fitness manager and went back to personal training only, and I decided to stop drinking alcohol. Those two decisions coincided with more time and flexibility in my schedule, better energy, and greater productivity. They also came with a pretty noticeable pay cut and lots of peer pressure from friends, but I was committed to throwing the boulder, not a pebble, and knew I had to be okay with some sacrifices.

The idea that you can make one or two decisions and send your life down a totally different path seems overly simplistic and impossibly scary at the same time. Is change really that easy? Maybe—if you make the right decisions, *fulcrum decisions*, that move the biggest boulders and have the greatest impact on multiple parts of your life. But that's also the scary part. How do you know if they're the right decisions?

Still, this perspective gives people a lot of hope. Changing your life can seem like an enormous lift. There are so many decisions to make that it's easy to end up with "decision fatigue" and avoid making any. But then you think about the fact that a few new choices can send you in a completely different direction, and it doesn't seem as overwhelming. If you can make the right calls in the right areas, it's like hitting the perfect combination on a lockbox that opens up a new future.

CALLING BULLSHIT

We like to think we make decisions for rational reasons. We don't. We make them for emotional reasons and then justify our choices after the fact by talking about data, logic, and cause and effect. That's why human beings suck at making pivotal choices: we're thinking with our hearts and heads, not our intuition. If we looked at our choices through the lens of what we're trying to avoid, what we're trying to deny, or what we're trying to hold on to, we'd be a lot better at overcoming our biases and making the decisions we already know we need to make.

HOW DO YOU CHOOSE?

Of course, the hardest thing is knowing which decisions will have the maximum impact on your life. First off, they're probably not decisions that seem dramatic and require inhuman willpower. Saying, "I'm going to work out every day for a year" or "I'm going to invest 50 percent of my take-home pay" doesn't get it done. Yes, those decisions *would* change your life—if you followed through. But those are such drastic and unrealistic moves that the odds of you being successful are slim.

Instead, fulcrum decisions tend to be decisions that compound, meaning their consequences magnify each other. Let's say you decide to hire a kick-ass personal trainer to help you get fit. Working with that trainer not only helps you stay on course for your fitness goals but also helps you sleep better, feel more confident, look better, and have more energy. Being more confident and having more energy leads to more fun in the bedroom and better performance at work, leading to a promotion to a leadership role and more money. One decision winds up changing your fitness, health, appearance, sex life, self-confidence, career, and income.

Or suppose you decide to do what I did years ago and remove alcohol from your life. Alcohol never controlled my life, but when I would drink, I'd never have just one . . . or two for that matter. Drinking, my drinking social circle, and time involved with drinking consumed a lot of my weekends. When I stopped drinking, I not only became healthier, was better rested, and felt more confident and disciplined, but I also found myself gravitating toward different types of people—people who wanted what I wanted and who inspired me, including other entrepreneurs, early risers, and others giving alcohol a break. Imagine deciding to simply give up alcohol and finding that your mental health, judgment, discipline, and relationships improved as a result. That's the kind of decision I'm talking about.

The following are a few clues that a decision has the potential to send you down a completely different path:

- It's easy to see the ripple effect and other positive effects that could exist if you make this one decision.
- There's a substantial buy-in. You'll spend time and money or be faced with some sort of painful consequence if you backslide.
- It requires you to accept significant uncomfort.

Change comes at a price, and you can't avoid paying the toll.

THE EMPOWERING DIFFERENCE BETWEEN "I CAN'T" AND "I'M NOT"

When you finally figure out those pivotal decisions, other factors come into play too. One of them is how you frame the decision to yourself and others. It's the difference between saying "I can't" and "I'm not." Let's stick with the alcohol-free example. Someone invites you to a Super Bowl party where there will be lots of beer and cocktails. If you tell the host, "*I can't* drink," it sounds like you're being restrained from doing something that you really want to do anyway. It almost invites friends to convince you to have just one drink.

But if you say, "I'm not drinking," that's a statement of identity. You're not straining at the leash to not do something; you've made an affirmative choice to live a different way. There's a world of difference between the two. Just contrast the impact of two ways of saying the same thing.

- "I can't eat meat" versus "I'm not eating meat."
- "I can't afford that" versus "I'm not going to buy that."

- "I can't go to happy hour tonight" versus "I'm not going to miss my workout class tonight."

One paints you as a victim; the other gives you agency and control. It's not hard to see which one is better for staying committed. Language matters. To make a big change, make sure the language you choose supports that change.

UNCOMFORTABLE TRUTH NO. 11

You already know what you need to do.

That feeling in the pit of your stomach as you read this chapter is a sign that there's at least one vital decision you already know you should make, but you haven't been able to pull the trigger. You may have even attempted it once before with little success. It might be ending a relationship or taking a new job, but your bias is blinding you to the need to make the hard call.

The telltale: Where have you been stuck at a level 2 frustration? What situation or problem have you been complaining about forever but haven't had the courage to take the leap on? That right there is your big decision.

FOCUS ON WHAT YOU'RE GAINING

Related to saying "I'm not" instead of "I can't" is the choice to put 90 percent of your focus on what you're getting from this big decision instead of what you're giving up. It's crucial to frame your decision in a positive way, not a negative way: "I'm alcohol-free" instead of "I'm giving up drinking." We've all had friends who, after they make a choice that they know is right and important, have a hard time getting past what they're losing. For example, someone who ended a bad relationship, and all they can do is mourn the fact that they're not going to have that person anymore. You may have to remind them, "You're focused only on the highlights, and we both know that wasn't what your relationship really was. You complained about them nonstop. You guys fought all the time and were becoming toxic to be around."

Instead of focusing on what you're giving up, focus on what you're gaining. If you're ending a dysfunctional relationship, you're getting your freedom and peace of mind back, and also the opportunity to find someone who has values more aligned to yours. If you're giving up fast food, you're gaining health, energy, and money because you're not going to spend fifty bucks a week on crap. If you quit your lousy job, you might be losing a steady paycheck, but you're gaining the opportunity to choose something better and more fulfilling for your time and future.

How can you frame your last big decision based on what you gained and not what you gave up?

LOW-HANGING WINS

Remember "stacking proof"? There are other things you can stack. I also teach "stacking wins," piling up small victories until they add up to something big. We've talked about winning your morning. We've talked about winning your week. Well, after you make a big, potentially life-changing decision, it's also really important to log some quick wins that help you say, "Hey, I'm doing the thing I said I would do!"

The reason to go after quick wins is because you're starting on a path of major change, and at the beginning you're most vulnerable to buyer's remorse—the impulse to backslide and decide you're not ready to break up, quit your job, or give up booze. Quick wins—getting your LLC and business credit card set up, filling your weekend mornings with something that reiterates how good it feels not to be hungover—help calm your nerves, keep your energy high, and reinforce that you can do this.

RELENTLESS FOLLOW-THROUGH

Finally, once you've made that big decision and framed it properly, none of it matters without *relentless* follow-through. What comes next, and what comes after that? Once the decision is made, what steps can you take to score some low-hanging wins and make it so there's no turning back? This is why making choices that can't be undone is so powerful. If going back isn't an option, you have no choice but to keep moving forward.

When you have the decision in front of you and you're confident it's the right one, ask yourself, "What do I do next? How do I lock this in?" Make a list of all the things you can do in the next three days to rack up small wins and prove to yourself that this is the right call.

ON THE OTHER SIDE

The confidence you're seeking, the opportunities you allow to pass you by, the person you want to become—it's all on the other side of one or two momentous decisions. Once you figure out what those decisions are, if you haven't already, you can tackle those challenges. This is a journey, and it's less about results than the mindset, character, and discipline you gain from the growth of change. This leap of faith isn't even about winning. It's about getting off the sidelines and into the game. If your decision turns out to be the wrong one, you try another. If you start and then backslide, you pick up and give it another shot. Nobody's keeping score, but I'll tell you this: you have no idea what unexpected doors your brave, determined, uncomfortable choices are going to open. That's the fun of change.

MOMENTUM BUILDERS

NOW: Tap into your intuition here. What's the first big, scary, and uncomfortable decision or choice that comes to mind when you think about creating a boulder's worth of ripple effects in your life? Write it down. Don't fight it. It's time to face the fear and lean in. It's time you give yourself a real shot at winning.

TODAY: Write down the two or three obstacles that have consistently kept you from growing in the ways you'd like or becoming the person you aspire to be. They could be habits, relationships, even addictions. Be honest with yourself and lean into the uncomfortable truth here. Once you think you know your biggest obstacles, talk with two or three trusted friends or confidants who know you well and have already been through the change you are about to make. Ask them if they've seen the same obstacles you're seeing now. Odds are, they have. They might even have talked to you about them before, but you didn't listen. Listen now and be open to their feedback.

PART IV

HOW TO AVOID THE "F*CK IT" BUTTON

THE SUNDAY SETUP

The minute you start taking any action that leads to uncomfort, you'll be tempted to hit the "Fuck It" button. Everybody has one, and I'm sure you've hit it a time or two, whether you were conscious of it or not. When you set a goal and make a promise to yourself, eventually, you're going to do what you know you shouldn't. You put $1,000 on the credit card you're trying to pay off. You snap at your spouse and do the exact opposite of what your therapist suggested. You skip a workout, then another. One mistake turns into two mistakes, and all of a sudden, you're standing in front of this gigantic red button with "Fuck It" written on it in huge block letters. Hitting the button is your way of saying, "I give up completely. I'm not going to shoot for 70 percent or even 50 percent of what I was trying to do. If I can't be perfect, I might as well quit."

Sounds pretty stupid when you read it like that, doesn't it? To me, succeeding 70 percent of the way at something is pretty good. The best quarterbacks in the NFL complete about 60 to 70 percent of their passes, and they get paid hundreds of millions of dollars. So something must be wrong.

It's not your goal. It's your all-or-nothing approach, the idea that you have to be perfect every day to make progress.

You don't. I don't win every day. Not even close. I have days when I'm tired or burned out and don't want to come up with an idea for my newsletter or go to the gym, and on some days that damn sabotaging little voice in my head wins. I'm not perfect. But the key is to not let yourself quit when you're not perfect. You don't need to stick to your plan perfectly to win. As I've said, the goal is to "win the day," which leads to winning the week, then the month, and then the year. You need to understand how quickly your life can improve if you just start winning more days than you lose.

Suppose you had planned to go to the gym four times this week, but it's Tuesday and you've already missed both days. You say, "Fuck it. This week is already a lost cause; I'll start next Monday." You're surrendering the week, which means you won't even do 25 percent of what you set out to do. You're guaranteeing yourself zero percent. (Do not confuse *Never Miss a Monday* with *Let me wait to restart until Monday.* They are far from the same.) Unfortunately, the impulse to quit because we get discouraged or disillusioned is pretty common.

Here's a chart that shows how detrimental this all-or-nothing mentality can be. Take two people with the same goal of working out four times

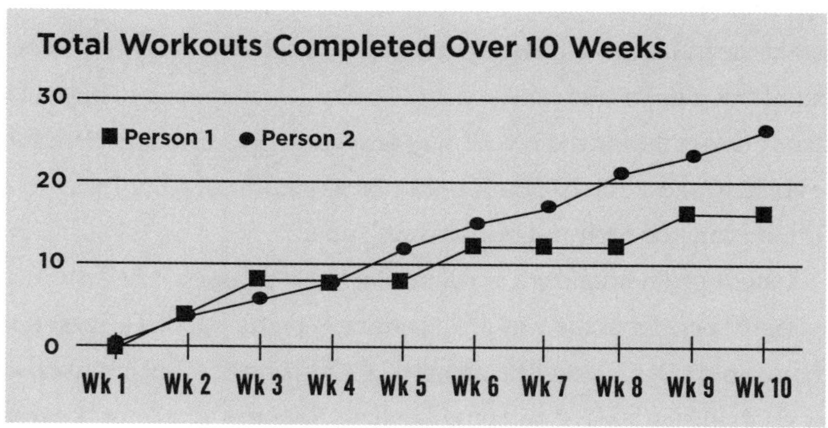

each week. One is the all-or-nothing type, while the other focuses on consistency, keeping momentum and doing the best they can each week.

In ten weeks, Person Number One had four perfect weeks but also had six weeks with zero workouts. I said it before and I'll say it again—most people don't realize that a zero day (or week) will diminish your progress far more than a perfect day (or week) will enhance it. Because of all the zero weeks, Person Number One ended up with 16 total workouts in ten weeks, an average of 1.6 workouts per week.

Person Number Two only had one perfect week, yet they prevented themselves from having any zero weeks. They ended up with 26 total workouts in ten weeks, an average of 2.6 workouts per week. That's ten more total workouts and an average of one more workout per week than Person Number One. Multiply this over a year, and you begin to see how quickly you can see results just by being consistent, keeping momentum on your side, fighting like hell to avoid the Fuck It button, and allowing no zero weeks.

The Sunday Setup (which pairs nicely with Never Miss a Monday) is a way to avoid those zero weeks and stay consistent, and I'm going to teach you how to use it.

BE PATIENT WITH YOUR GOALS BUT NOT WITH YOUR EFFORT

One of the big reasons I see people slamming down on the "Fuck It" button is that they're too ambitious with their time horizons. Some folks set goals with the finish line at six months or a year, but when it comes to correcting bad habits or rewriting limiting beliefs you've fed for the last ten years, six months might as well be a lifetime. We can't imagine where we'll be or what we'll be doing over that long a time. I like to get my clients to commit to a specific program of change over ninety days because that's long enough to see substantial results while being short enough to maintain a sense of urgency.

Still, even then I'm more likely to break things down to one week at a time. Winning the week is everything because that's a manageable time frame. It's not overwhelming to plan to change your eating or spending habits for seven days, then do it again and again.

It's important to find a way to stay disciplined and focused for those short sprints. Progress is progress, and it mostly doesn't matter how you get where you're going. A lot of people would rather run ten all-out sprints than run two miles in a single day because they feel better checking the small boxes and getting closer to the finish line. Setting smaller goals over a shorter time horizon lets you build up momentum, and that's what keeps you going.

Stop looking at the big picture. The big picture lies to you and tells you that you have to be a superhero. You don't. You just have to be one rep or one choice better than you were the day before. A win is a win. If you're only doing 50 percent of what you set out to do but you're doing it over a long period, you're still making big progress and your effort is still compounding. I certainly want you to aim higher than that, but hey, losing half a pound a week for a year still means you lose twenty-six pounds. That's like removing a backpack full of books from your shoulders! The key is to be patient with your goals but not with your effort. Your effort must be urgent!

Patience may be a virtue, but if leveraged incorrectly, it will become another comfortable built-in excuse that prevents you from seeing results.

One of the other tools you can use to keep yourself from hitting the button is *regret*. Regret hits when we mash the "Fuck It" button because we're bored, frustrated, or whatever; then we look back a year later and say to ourselves, "Why didn't I stay in that night school class? I'd have my degree now!" or "Why did I quit working on my book? If I'd kept writing, I'd be a published author by now!" It's that feeling that we could have gotten so much closer to our goal if we'd just made one different decision—not to quit.

One of the first things that I do with a client who has a history of hitting the dreaded button is help them figure out where their *off-ramp* is. What makes them suddenly think about quitting? After how long does it typically happen?

What makes you lose interest? What triggers thoughts such as, "I've been consistent for three weeks, two weeks, a month, or six weeks, but this is where I start to self-sabotage"? The four-to-six-week mark seems to be a common speed bump. Does that sound familiar? The honeymoon phase is over, and it's become clear that reaching your goal isn't going to be as fast as influencers make it look on Instagram. It's not sexy to eat clean anymore, and you're dying for a slice of pizza. Walking on the treadmill feels hard. Signing that first client is taking longer than you expected and showing up on social media has lost its shine. This is the moment you contemplate quitting. This is your off-ramp.

If I can find out where that moment is for each person, that's when we can double down and start to put some mechanisms in place to help them get past those moments and avoid the regret of looking back and saying, "Oh, if only . . ."

CALLING BULLSHIT

Nothing forces you to quit. You allow yourself to take the off-ramp and quit. By taking ownership of that decision and not blaming past failures on external circumstances, you reclaim the power to make things different. By blaming something or someone for your quitting, you're setting yourself up to do the same thing in the future. But by taking ownership of your choices, you increase the odds that you won't make the same mistake next time.

WATCH OUT FOR LANDMINES

A winning Sunday Setup is one part awareness, one part confidence, and one part reducing friction. Friction is anything that can potentially reduce your momentum or start you rationalizing and otherwise finding reasons why you can't do what you promised yourself you would do. You're not only making things easier but making them procrastination-proof and excuse-proof too. Here are some examples:

- Prepping ingredients for the coming week's healthy meals so all you have to do is grab and cook
- Dumping all the booze down the drain to reduce the temptation to have a drink
- Setting up autodeposit that automatically takes money from your checking account and invests it into your stock portfolio

But the core of the Sunday Setup is being aware of what's coming up next week and planning to ensure it doesn't derail your progress. Most people could probably be twice as productive—maybe even five times as productive—just by planning ahead to avoid traps in the coming week so they can get things done—and even have extra time on their hands. Too many people wake up with no idea what their day is going to look like. They stroll into work with big ambitions to *Get. Shit. Done.* Then they look at their calendar, and somehow, it takes them by surprise. "I have a call at eleven. Really? Shit, the kids have a dentist appointment this morning? Today is Susie's birthday, and we're all going to happy hour. I knew that, so why did I book my workout for six o'clock tonight?"

When you don't plan for the coming week, you set yourself up to fail. You're choosing to play defense instead of offense. You're taking your goal and putting it in a place where it doesn't have any chance to survive, like a houseplant left in a dark room. Planning the week out lets you avoid *landmines*. Landmines are anything that can blow up your week, blow up your day, or blow up your schedule. And the funny thing about landmines is that we set most of them.

But with a little bit of forethought and awareness, you can avoid a lot of those landmines. On Sunday, you calendar the coming week and account for every possible landmine: a flight, a meeting, an early morning, a doctor's appointment, a late-night brainstorming session, taking the kids to their recital. You might have scheduled them two or three weeks ago, but if you don't look ahead using this Sunday process, something will surprise you and throw you off. Sometimes that's all it takes to derail your week and have you looking for the Fuck It button, and vowing to start again next Monday.

Here's the thing: *a landmine is only a threat if it goes off.* If you catch it and plan for it so it doesn't interfere with your workout, therapy session, or whatever, you defuse it. I love catching something that would've totally messed up my Thursday if I hadn't looked ahead and caught it four days in advance. I can preplan when to get my workouts in or swap my rest days if needed, account for the fact that I might be on the road during a coaching call and need reliable Wi-Fi, and plan time to just rest and do nothing. You can save yourself a ton of frustration—and keep yourself from mashing the big red button—with some Sunday planning.

UNCOMFORTABLE TRUTH NO. 12

Sundays don't have to be scary.

Everybody knows about the so-called Sunday Scaries, the anxiety and dread you feel on Sunday evening because you know on Monday you have to go back to a job that you may dread. But the Sunday Scaries actually have little to do with your job and more to do with not having control. If you follow the Sunday Setup plan to the letter and execute it, you'll dramatically reduce your dread and anxiety. That's because you're taking control of your week and making affirmative choices to get better, richer, stronger, and smarter. You'll enjoy your Sundays a lot more, and you might even look forward to Mondays!

WEEKS ARE WON ON SUNDAY

The Sunday Setup is all about playing offense with your life. Instead of letting the events of the coming week control you, you're *taking* control. You're making positive choices and deciding not only what to say yes to but also, more importantly, what to say no to. Creating your week's plan should only take about thirty minutes, but it will be the most impactful thirty minutes of your week. Just think, this half hour of awareness and positive planning might be the only thing preventing you from making the big changes that have eluded you in the past!

The Sunday Setup has eight steps:

1. **Create an environment.** The energy we show up with and put into something, especially when setting intentions, really matters. Create a positive physical and sensory environment for writing out your Sunday Setup plan. To quote the Broadway masterpiece *Hamilton*, this is The Room Where It Happens. Figure out the room, seating, music, and lighting that inspire you and enable you to cruise through the plan in thirty minutes. This includes how you write out your plan, whether that's on paper by hand or on a tablet or laptop. I've always enjoyed using a blue-and-red erasable pen and the same notebook for all

fifty-two weeks, but try both and decide what you enjoy more. Also, block out a set time every Sunday to plan. That's your Do Not Disturb time. One piece of advice: Don't make your Sunday Setup the last thing you do before bed. You'll be rushed and less invested. Instead, do it in the morning and enjoy the rest of your day, knowing you're all planned out and ready for the coming week.

2. **Choose a mantra.** What pushes your emotional buttons and gets you fired up? What quote, saying, number, or other device do you need to keep you focused and dialed in all week long? This is something that keeps you going when you're tempted to give up during a dull Thursday workout or a long meeting. It could be a picture that reminds you why this goal is so important, a dollar amount showing you how close you are to saving a down payment for a house, or dozens of other things. It just needs to fire you up to stay focused and win the week ahead.
3. **Review.** I describe this as "watching game film." What did you get right last week, and how can you do it again? What tripped you up last week, and how can you prevent it this week? What was the most important lesson you learned last week that will allow you to do better this week? If you run into the same potential landmine as you did last week, what will you do differently? Keep this positive. Don't focus only on everything you did wrong. Pick one mistake or poor decision and map out how you'll do better if faced with it again. The goal is to learn, get better every week, and not make the same poor choice (or excuse) twice. That's fifty-two chances to improve.

4. **Scan for landmines.** With your calendar or schedule in hand, mentally walk through your next two weeks, looking for things that could add friction or derail your progress: calls or meetings, social events, nights out, trips, birthdays, and so on. Move what you can, reschedule others, find a babysitter if you need to, or have food delivered. Looking two weeks ahead gives you two chances to catch landmines before they blow up and cause any damage.
5. **Prioritize IPAs and NMTs.** IPAs are "income-producing activities." If you're a business owner or entrepreneur, these are things that make your business money. These tasks must be prioritized. For everyone else, this could be a side hustle, a second stream of income, or steps to help you land your next promotion. NMTs are "needle-moving tasks." These are activities or multi-step projects that help you progress toward your next target. Use your NMT list to break those bigger projects down into smaller action steps to avoid confusion and procrastination. Both are essential to having a great, winning week. Keep your IPA and NMT lists short; more is not better, and you can easily find yourself overwhelmed. What things can you do next week that will improve your finances, career, relationships, health, or happiness? These should be nonnegotiable, specific things you have full control over. "Apply for jobs" doesn't cut it. "Friday at 4:00 p.m., update my résumé so that on Monday I can send it to the three great jobs I found on Indeed.com" is more like it.
6. **Have a "TWO" do list.** TWO stands for "this week only." If you have a running to-do list for your whole life, I'll

guarantee you two things: it's too long, and some things have been on there for months. Right? You need to trim your list so you can aim to accomplish everything on it, and the best way to do this is to trim the list and prioritize what is urgent for this week only. Update your list to only include things that have to be completed in the coming week. It's fine to split the list into columns marked "Business" and "Personal," but be realistic. You're probably not going to complete a list twenty items long. Six items are reasonable, and if they're six things that have a positive impact on your health, wealth, or peace, even better. You will see much faster progress and feel much more disciplined if you can get comfortable with scheduling less but finishing more each week. With anything that doesn't have to be done next week, write it on the left side of the page as a long-term list and see if it fits into the following week. (Pro tip for a happy relationship: Run your personal list by your significant other to make sure your priorities for the week align with family needs or their honey-do list.)

7. **Schedule it.** This is the most important part of owning your week. This is where you lock in a specific day and time on your schedule for your to-do items, your IPAs, and your NMTs. No, there won't be enough time for everything, which means you'll have to either discard some activities or move them to your long-term to-do list. You're making time for what's really important to you and things that will move the needle. A couple of tips: Plan time for rest, fun, and relationships. Nobody can be at work or the gym 168 hours a week. Calendar more time than you think you'll

need for the most important tasks. You'll appreciate the white space if you complete them quicker.

8. **Execute.** High performers are consistent in their execution. Look at your Sunday Setup plan every morning to make sure you're still on track. Celebrate small wins and give yourself some grace if you fall short. Stay organized, stay prioritized, and work the plan. Every workday should begin with an income-producing or needle-moving activity. I like to use the four quarters of the day we spoke about earlier to help decide when I will accomplish certain tasks.

That's it. Use Wednesday as your midweek checkpoint and gauge how well you're executing and hitting your to-dos, IPAs, and NMTs. Friday is another important day and can be the difference between an average or "big win" week. Don't coast to the finish line and pack it in, or you'll wind up with a Sunday Setup filled with unaccomplished tasks from the previous week. Take pride in finishing strong and block off some time on Fridays to check everything you can off your to-do list.

High performers aggressively play offense, dominating the three days—Sunday, Monday, and Friday—when most people coast and settle for the minimum. Sundays are now for your strategic setup. Never Miss a Monday is your new mantra, and you'll intentionally finish strong and dominate Fridays.

Win those three important days and watch how easily you begin to build momentum and win your weeks!

MOMENTUM BUILDERS

NOW: Figure out where and how you'll write out each Sunday Setup. Do you need a quiet room, or are you happy planning at the local coffee shop? Do you do your best thinking first thing Sunday morning or after some coffee and a walk? With music or silence? Outside or at your desk? Now set a reminder in your phone for this coming Sunday morning to attempt your first Sunday Setup. Give yourself sixty minutes for this first attempt so that you can thoroughly go through each step.

TODAY: Take a look at the rest of your week and map out any landmines—outings, family commitments, parties, doctors' appointments, and so on. Anything that could be a bump in the road to your momentum. Write out your plan for keeping those landmines from interfering with your progress, and reference this list when doing your first setup.

CHAPTER 13

WILLPOWER'S FOR SUCKERS

There's a wall out there. When you close your eyes, you can see it, day or night. It's not a high or a particularly thick wall—at least not yet. You can tell that it's not strong and that with a little bit of effort, you could probably punch a hole right through it. That wall is what stands between you and the "Fuck It" button. It's the only thing that keeps you from mashing that stupid button whenever you feel discouraged or when you have a craving for something—dopamine, food, sex, spending money—that you just can't resist anymore.

The wall must be made of your willpower, right? Wrong. But we'll get to that. First, I want to talk to you about Steve Jobs and Mark Zuckerberg.

Jobs, the great Apple cofounder, was famous for a lot of things, and one of them was wearing the same outfit every day: jeans and a black turtleneck. When asked about this odd habit, Jobs said that wearing the same clothes every day meant he had fewer decisions to make—and since he was building what would become the world's most valuable company, he had a lot of decisions to make. Years later, Zuckerberg, cofounder and

CEO of Facebook and Meta, would don his own "uniform" for the same reason. For these two tech giants, wearing the same stuff was a way to reduce decision fatigue.

Experience suggests (and science supports this idea) that our ability to make choices—especially if they require us to do what we'd rather not do or say no to what we really want—is finite. Call it willpower if you want to, but it's like a muscle: work it hard enough, long enough, and it gets fatigued. Eventually, it fails. But different choices "weigh" different amounts. Choices that give us what we want or that are neutral, such as choosing heads or tails in a coin flip, don't fatigue our willpower very much. But the more the choice takes us into uncomfort, the heavier it is. Choosing between water and iced tea at a restaurant is like lifting a two-pound dumbbell; choosing to get out of your warm bed at five o'clock on a freezing winter morning to put on your shoes and get to the gym for a one-hour workout can be like deadlifting a bulldozer.

After you have your Sunday Setup worked out and your plan and environment in order, you're still going to face tough choices. Sorry, but we already agreed that change is hard. So why not reduce decision fatigue every place you can, even by a small amount? I personally don't wear the same thing all the time, mostly because my lovely wife is very fashionable and helps me make sure my clothes match. However, I do have six of the exact same shirts in different colors, and I do eat the same first two meals almost every day. People ask me, "How do you eat eggs every day?" Well, I do get sick of them sometimes, but not enough to add unnecessary decisions to my day. Plus making them is part of my routine. I cook them up, and by the time I even start to contemplate, "Do I want eggs or not?" they're already made and in front of me. So I eat them.

That's important for me because it removes friction. It automates two decisions during my day. I know my chosen meals are healthy. I know they have enough calories and give me good energy. I get the healthy mix of what I want. Mostly, I like the fact that I don't have to think about what to eat. I know that I won't feel lethargic and that I won't be wasting time when I cook or shop.

CALLING BULLSHIT

People who automate many parts of their lives must live boring lives, right? False. By reducing the time and mental energy spent on routine decisions, people can allocate more resources to planning, strategizing, and implementing more impactful long-term goals. This can lead to better overall performance, happiness, and higher achievements in both the personal and professional spheres. Automating decisions can also reduce the stress and anxiety associated with choice overload.

THE GOLDEN FREAKIN' TICKET

The point of me telling you that I eat eggs every morning is to finally, just maybe, drive a stake through the heart of a myth that's been discouraging people from trying to make big changes in their lives since . . . well, since forever. Here's the truth:

Welcoming uncomfort and making important, lasting change is not about willpower.

Willpower isn't the most important factor in determining whether you reach your goals. Willpower is simply a matter of getting yourself to do what you don't want to do. But even then, it's not quite that simple.

For instance, a German study tracked 205 people for one week. These participants were given phones that would randomly send them questions about their desires, temptations, and self-control in the moment. The people who said they were the best at self-control—the ones who most agreed with statements such as "I am good at resisting temptations"—reported experiencing fewer temptations throughout the week. In other words, the people who said they had terrific self-control hardly needed to use it.*

This means that people who claim to have high levels of willpower or self-control generally avoid testing it. How? One way is to make doing some of the things they don't want to do relatively enjoyable. That could be as simple as working through a task you aren't super keen on with good energy and a smile. I remember the first time I shoveled snow while listening to music. My toleration and enjoyment of a not-so-fun task increased significantly, dare I say I didn't mind it at all. All because my focus was removed from the task of shoveling, and was put on the new music I got to enjoy. Another way is to structure their lives in a way that removes temptation and gives them no choice but to do things they want to do.

Your struggle with self-doubt and confidence will continue until you can get yourself to do the thing you know you need to do, even when you don't feel like doing it.

Read that statement as many times as it takes to sink in, because that right there is the Golden Freakin' Ticket to massive, positive change in your life! This is the *only* difference between disciplined and undisciplined people. This is *everything.* I want your willpower to be the least important factor in executing your Sunday Setup and making progress toward your goals.

Yes, I'm talking about changing *habits.* I can hear you groan, and I get it. Changing habits isn't easy. If it was, everybody would be exactly who they want to be and where they want to be. But you don't become who you want to become and then change your habits. It's the other way around. New habits come first. Your habits determine who you become. The key

* Hofmann, W., R. F. Baumeister, G. Förster, and K. D. Vohs. "Everyday temptations: an experience sampling study of desire, conflict, and self-control." *J Pers Soc Psychol* 102, no. 6 (2012): 1318-35. https://doi.org/10.1037/a0026545. Epub 2011 Dec 12. PMID: 22149456.

to success is to make willpower not the most important factor in changing harmful habits and establishing new ones but rather the *least* important.

That brings us back to the wall. That wall between you and the "Fuck It" button is your willpower. It's weak and fragile because willpower *is* weak and fragile. What we're going to talk about is how to build two more big, strong walls between you and that button. That way, you have to break through those other walls first, exhausting yourself before you are able to break through the willpower wall and press that destructive button. Those other reinforcing walls are as follows:

- **Autopilot**
- **Discipline**

Those are the walls that make it much harder for you to get to the button. What good is willpower then? Well, I'll make you a deal. If you use all your willpower to build up these outer walls that help you avoid temptation, in the future you'll barely need to use your willpower at all.

UNCOMFORTABLE TRUTH NO. 13:

Self-discipline trumps natural talent.

Study after study has shown that people who rank higher in self-control, self-discipline, and delaying gratification do better in school, advance faster in their careers, are wealthier, and are happier. In college students, self-discipline is more important than IQ in predicting academic success. So if you can develop more self-control even in small areas, you stand a chance at improving your results in many others. If you're not getting the results in your life that you want, it might be because your self-discipline still sucks.

AUTOPILOT . . . IN THE RIGHT DIRECTION

Autopilot is when things happen without you having to think about them. But putting everything on autopilot is not necessarily a good thing. Autopilot is only useful when the plane is flying in the right direction. The goal is to put the things that help you on autopilot while taking the things that distract you and restrict your progress off the table as much as possible.

Brushing your teeth is an example of autopilot. You probably don't choose which tooth to brush. You just pick up the brush and start brushing. You've done it so many times that it's automatic. Another example is your commute to work. If you've been working in the same place for years, you don't plan out your route and think about what turns to make. System one, the automatic part of your brain, takes over and gets you to work without you thinking about it. There's nothing wrong with those kinds of autopilot habits because they're not very consequential. Even if there is a detour or you take a wrong turn on the way to work, it's an easy fix and barely disrupts your podcast listening.

But autopilot can be a problem when your habits get you into trouble. What if you want to quit drinking, but you're in the habit of going to happy hour every Thursday with your friends from work? If you say yes and show up without thinking about it, you're likely going to drink because you're testing your willpower beyond its breaking point. Or let's say you and your partner put your kids to bed every night, but as soon as the kids are asleep, you both flop down on the couch, take out your phones, and don't speak to each other for an hour. That's intimate, quiet time you could use to talk and connect, but you don't because your evening routine with your phones is on autopilot. This autopilot routine is not flying your plane in the direction of a fulfilling and deeply connected marriage.

By becoming aware of all the negative things you're doing on autopilot, you can change things. Can you adopt new habits to stop you from doing counterproductive things on autopilot? Sometimes. If you try, start small. Saying, "I'm going to change this habit and stop doing what I've been doing the same way for the last four years" sounds unrealistic because it is. So start by changing a habit that's low-hanging fruit. For instance, if you have a bad habit of always being late to meet the same friend for lunch, start setting an alarm to leave fifteen minutes earlier than usual.

However, for most habits, you'll get a better bang for your buck if you take the choice out of your hands altogether. In other words, automate positive actions that promote progress and growth. As speaker and brand expert Rory Vaden says, "Automation is to your time what compound interest is to your money." He's spot-on. What may take some extra time and energy up front will pay off in spades down the road once these good habits and time-savers are on autopilot. My autopilot of making the same two meals every day has compounded into saving me hours each week on decisions and added up to week after week of feeling great about my nutrition. Even the best plan is useless if you blow it off, so automate what you can. Make it as difficult as possible to cheat or quit. Automation takes willpower out of the equation and will reduce your chances of failure.

What kinds of things can you, and should you, put on autopilot?

- Setting up an autodeposit from your checking account into a stock portfolio, 401(k), or some sort of savings
- Attending your workout class or training session at the same time each day
- Deciding together with your partner that the third Friday of each month is date night
- Eating the same healthy breakfast from Monday to Friday that you know will give you great energy and help you build muscle

Autopilot can help you develop new habits in a way that just making better choices can't always do because it takes choice out of the equation. Your investments just accrue; date nights are protected because they're already on the calendar. By the way, this is what the most successful high achievers do—they reduce decision fatigue by removing the option of making poor choices. They know they already have enough choices to make, so why make everything harder by playing some dumb "I have more willpower than you" game?

How do you put things on autopilot? Like this:

1. Mentally walk through your typical day at work and at home, and identify the places where you're not getting optimal results: exercise, grooming, transportation, shopping, work communication, paying bills, and so on. Make a list of the top four or five areas where you think small improvements could make a big difference.
2. Think about ways you could automate those activities in some way. For example, do you have time to cook healthy meals at home, or do you end up grabbing crap a lot of the time because you can't get to the store or have no time to cook? Maybe signing up for one of those ready-to-cook, grocery delivery services would make sense for you. Or if you're constantly paying late fees on your household bills, what about signing up for free bill pay from your bank?
3. Put autopilot in place in at least three areas and watch how those areas begin to compound

However, autopilot is a two-way street. There are some parts of anyone's life that should not be on autopilot. Here's how and where to take things *off* autopilot:

1. Make a short list of some current habits that are on autopilot that shouldn't be. Where are you self-sabotaging and keeping yourself stuck because of your "normal routine," which is actually more like a "rut"? What are you doing each week that you know you shouldn't be doing? Highlight a few of those areas.
2. Put a "friction plan" in place to make those bad habits intentional and difficult. The friction should help reduce temptation. Force yourself to grab the steering wheel with these and be consciously deliberate with your actions.

Think of the dials and sliders on a high-end audio system. You switch things on and off and move things around until you find a combination that gives you the sound you want. For me, eating eggs, nuts, and fruit every day is great but isn't possible if I don't have the food in my fridge and pantry, so grocery shopping or delivery also needs to be on autopilot. That's one less thing I have to think about and one less test of my willpower. The few times I ran out of eggs for one reason or another, I ended up eating grilled cheese and chips because I'm human and chose food based on my current mood and emotions instead of my usual autopilot.

Autopilot is the first wall between you and the "Fuck It" button and will protect you from your biggest threat: yourself.

ENCOURAGING YOU TO SUCCEED VERSUS TEMPTING YOU TO FAIL

The second wall is discipline, but here's where people make a common mistake: *they confuse willpower and discipline.* Willpower is *not* the same as discipline. Willpower is about resisting what you're not supposed to do but secretly want to do. You want to eat that frozen pizza even though you swore you were going keto. You want to go over to your ex's place for a booty call even though you know it'll lead to regret. With willpower, you're grinding against your desires and using up your energy reserves.

Discipline is about doing what you've planned to do because you put yourself in a position where that's all you can do. Again, you're taking choice out of the picture, but this time you're doing it by making a *different* choice that doesn't expose you to temptation. Willpower is dependent on how you feel—how well you slept, how hungry you are, what kind of mood you're in, how much stress you're under. Also, we tend to expect willpower to show up when we're already backsliding and two steps down the road of bailing on our commitments. Not discipline. Discipline is having a plan and sticking to it.

Super successful people don't drop themselves into dangerous situations day after day and pray that willpower will show up when they need it. That's like searching for fun things on Amazon and then daring yourself not to buy anything. It's stupid, and they know it. Instead, they choose different situations. If you're a man trying to repair a rocky marriage and you're feeling tempted to cheat on your wife, you probably shouldn't go to strip clubs by yourself while conveniently forgetting to wear your wedding ring. That option should be off the table for you, period. If you're a woman in the same position, you probably shouldn't text your recently single ex just to catch up and see how he's doing. You block his number. If you're trying to lose weight and you have a sweet tooth, you don't go hang out in a donut shop.

Got it? Discipline means you *do not* unnecessarily test your willpower. A big reason why disciplined people stay disciplined is that they tempt themselves less. It's not magic; it's your environment.

Want to drastically improve your discipline? Create an environment that encourages you to succeed instead of constantly tempting you to fail.

This is how you deal with bad habits that are too hard to change simply by being aware of them. If your favorite healthy restaurant is right next door to your favorite ice cream shop, start eating somewhere else. If you're trying to quit drinking alcohol, you tell your girlfriends that you'd love to meet up on Saturday morning instead of Saturday night, and preferably somewhere that isn't bottomless brunch. You're creating an environment that reduces temptation, a schedule that reduces temptation, a refrigerator that reduces temptation.

We all know ourselves really well, so we know the loopholes we're likely to crawl through if we give ourselves the chance. For instance, I become a Cookie Monster around chocolate chip cookies. I can put the cookies on the back shelf, but if I still know where I put them, I'll still know how to get them. That's the "Fuck It" button. Discipline is getting rid of the damn cookies—or, better yet, not buying them in the first place! What makes actors playing superheroes and investors who become millionaires so awesome is that they construct their lives so it's nearly impossible for them to hit the "Fuck It" button in the areas they care about. Believe it or not, I don't consider myself highly disciplined. I am, however, really good at putting myself in environments that encourage me to succeed, instead of tempting me to cave.

HOW LONG DOES IT TAKE TO BUILD A HABIT?

Autopilot and discipline give you two ways to change habits that don't rely on willpower. That's awesome. With both working for you, you've got two thick walls between you and that damned button. See how much harder it's gonna be for you to push it? Suppose you have a stressful day at work and you come home wanting to binge on pizza and beer. Sorry—you don't have either one in the house! You could go to the store, but then you open your fridge and see the food from your home delivery meal service in there, and you're like, "Well, shit, I already paid for this food, and I'm supposed to eat well, so . . ." You fire up the cooktop and make yourself a healthy meal.

It's not heroic. There's no titanic battle of wills here. And that's the point. Willpower is for suckers. It weakens. But with discipline and autopilot in place, you're a lot less likely to make a choice you'll regret later.

One of the best ways to summarize this comes from the great NBA sharpshooter Steph Curry, quoting his Davidson College coach, Bob McKillop. Bob answered the age-old question, "How long does it take to build a new habit?" by saying, "It's not about how long it takes until you get it right. It's about how long it takes before you can't get it wrong."

Go easy on yourself. We make too many decisions every day to expect ourselves to make the right choice all the time. That's why these other options exist. Choosing a good decision over a bad one is great, but creating a situation where the good decision is your only option is even better.

MOMENTUM BUILDERS

NOW: Identify one habit or situation where you have been tempting yourself to fail instead of encouraging yourself to succeed. What change can you make to your environment? What can you add or remove to make it easier to follow through successfully? Write the changes down.

TODAY: Mentally walk through a typical month and plot those choices that put you in situations and environments where your willpower is severely tested. Don't forget the weekends, when most of us have an increase in freedom and decisions due to different schedules, routines, and discipline. Now write out how you could change your choices so you're not in those situations at all. Be sure to consider possible challenges—ticked-off friends, initial inconvenience, and other situations such as this. How can you give yourself the best opportunity to succeed?

ADVERSITY NOW = ADVANTAGE LATER

When you talk about adversity, eventually, the conversation has to come back to COVID-19. The pandemic was an unprecedented event, maybe the most frightening and difficult thing most of us have ever gone through. It was difficult for me because I'm a very structured and routine-oriented person, and COVID-19 flipped just about every routine I had upside down. I had to find ways not only to overcome the adversity I was experiencing but also to help the people who looked to me to move past their own issues.

The biggest challenge was probably the lack of discipline that came with isolation. How disciplined are you when you don't have to get up, get dressed, and go to the gym or the office? When you can lounge around the house all day watching Netflix in your sweatpants, do you? I did a lot of extra group coaching during COVID-19, and on my Zoom sessions from that time, I remember everyone saying, "I can't wait to get back to normal." I told everybody, "I'm with you. I can't wait for things to open back up a little bit too." But I also advised them that, before rushing back to "normal," they should really use the time as an opportunity to think about how well "normal" was working for them pre-pandemic.

Was your idea of normal burning you out? Were you healthy back when things were normal? Did you like your long commute? Were you happy most days? My position was that the adversity we were all experiencing in the depths of the pandemic could give us an advantage later because this was an opportunity to make big changes and set up the life we wanted going forward. Now if we're being honest, most people didn't follow through on the plans they made during COVID-19 lockdowns. They went right back to the same bad habits they had before. But . . . *some people did make changes*! They've negotiated the ability to work remotely now a few days each week instead of being stuck in an office full time. They've relocated and started new careers, with some even starting their own businesses. They've reinvented themselves physically, mentally, and spiritually. So it's possible. Similar to how we talked about being in a rut in the previous chapter, COVID or not, I don't think there's ever a bad time to re-evaluate your normal.

The people who turned the challenges of COVID-19 into positive change are an example of my principle of "adversity now equals advantage later." When you face hardship—when you work until you drop at the gym, when you put in twenty-four-hour days to get a new company off the ground—you get stronger, wiser, and more resilient. That makes it easier down the line to reach your most important goals.

I don't want to suggest that some people handle adversity easily. Hard times or hard work will always be hard. When you want to change your body or reverse twenty years of bad financial decisions, that's still a challenge you wish you didn't have to face. But the people who stay disciplined, the ones who eventually get to those huge goals that the rest of us envy, are the ones who say, "I know I need to go through this, and I know that when I get where I want to be, I'll look back at this hard time as pivotal, so let's do it. Let's keep moving forward."

I relate this to my favorite part of all superhero movies, the "origin story." Superhero stories usually involve the characters going through early adversity to gain their life-altering power and purpose later on. Batman saw his parents killed in front of him and was forced to leverage his deepest fears in order to make himself the perfect symbol against evil. Spider-Man got bitten by a radioactive spider and then lost his uncle Ben. Wolverine endured the agony of getting adamantium drilled into his skeleton, only to find out he was only a lab experiment who would be killed and used for his DNA. Superhero or not, what you're able to put yourself through defines what you can achieve. So let's do this.

CALLING BULLSHIT

You can't just overcome adversity by snapping your fingers—and not all adversity is created equal. This is similar to the "Action Builds Confidence" chapter, where we noted how taking small versus big actions will give you a relative amount of confidence in return. If you have been through some major adversity (or trauma) in your life, you may not experience the advantage immediately afterward, like they do in the movies. It may take years. Realizing some of the personal advantages of going through that tough year when I was sixteen didn't show up until years later when I was ready to look back on those experiences from a different perspective. When it did, it allowed me to appreciate the advantage I gained from them and then use that power for good. I'm here to tell you that you also have that power. You just need the right perspective so it becomes your catalyst and advantage instead of the anchor holding you back and keeping you stuck.

RECYCLING YOUR PAIN

We are at our best when we're striving for something or overcoming obstacles. Give us too much comfort and we end up sitting on the couch eating Taco Bell and watching reruns of *Friends*. That's why the concept of uncomfort is so important. Too much ease and comfort make us lazy and complacent, which will never lead to feeling fulfilled. But when you give us something to push against, we not only get stronger and tougher, but we also remember what we were like *before*.

For instance, my back injury, while devastating at the time, has made me appreciate having a healthy body to explore and push to its limits. My memory of that miserable year won't allow me to take my fitness for granted. If you trace it back far enough, you could make the argument that my motivational speaking career stemmed from trying to be a great teammate while not being able to physically play or score points. *I still want to be a helpful teammate, so let me give a ton of high fives. Let me be really encouraging. Let me cheer up the guy who just made a mistake. Let me impact my team through my energy and enthusiasm.* That's when I realized my most valuable gift wasn't my physical strength but my ability to inspire through words, energy, and encouragement (and, of course, some tough love). My best character traits, as well as many of my core values and beliefs, all came through adversity.

So while you can't undo your pain, you can recycle it. Beautiful things start to occur when you evolve from the mindset of "I can't" to "I can't afford not to."

Both of those sophomore-year instances were painful moments that I could have played on repeat as excuses for the rest of my life as the reasons why I can't, won't be able to, or why others have it easier than me. Believe me—I did for a number of years, but eventually I got tired of fighting for my limiting beliefs, decided to stop playing the victim, and embraced the power of my origin story and unique perspective. I recycled my pain into my unique advantage—personally and to help others. It's those tough, dark times when you felt the most broken that you look back on later and realize that's when you found your own superpowers. That's where your advantage lies. Many of the most inspiring people on the planet have found a way to recycle their pain in the service of others.

You don't have to love adversity, but when you're in it, try to remember that if you can get through it, you will gain an advantage. Let that motivate you to get through the adversity faster because that means you get to the advantage faster. Challenges and circumstances that push you to your limits are the opportunity costs of life. If you ever start to doubt that you can make it through, remember this:

The universe will never give you more than you can handle—it just may be more than you expected.

You're probably familiar with the hero's journey or the heroic cycle. It's a basic storytelling device that you can find in stories as familiar as the *Harry Potter* series. "But wait," you might say to yourself, "I'm no hero." Yes, you are. You're the hero of your own story. Every one of us is. So it's important to look at your journey, from where you are today to where you want to go, as a hero's journey. Because the classic stages of that journey really do show up in your efforts to get in better shape, build a better career, or fix your finances. Take a look at the following major stages, and you'll see what I mean:

- **Discovery.** This is when you first change your environment, set your plan in motion, and try things you've never tried before. You're getting up at 5:00 a.m. for the first time. You're getting formal training in how to interview for a job. You're feeling awkward, getting deep into uncomfort, and learning all kinds of things about yourself.

- **Adversity.** Things are getting hard, and you're getting increasingly uncomfortable. Maybe you're working with a personal trainer who's leaving you in a gasping heap on the floor. Maybe you're going to interviews and feeling totally out of your league. You're pushing against your limits, working harder than ever, and wondering if you have what it takes.
- **Dark night.** This is the point where you're ready to quit. You're discouraged, doubting that you can do this, and looking for the "Fuck It" button. You might already have gotten results, but you can't see them. In a movie this would be the end of the second act, where the worst thing that could happen has happened. But the story's not over.
- **New strength.** Maybe on your own, maybe with the help of friends or family, or maybe with a coach or mentor, you find a way to get off the floor and take one more step. Slowly, you realize that you're already stronger, smarter, more skilled . . . *better*. Maybe you *can* do this. Now you see the results—the bigger biceps, the fatter bank account, the calls for a second interview—and realize yes, you're making progress.
- **Finish line.** You made it! You reached your goal, and you feel incredible. You're changed forever, and you know that while the next challenge might be harder, you're more confident that you can handle it.

That's the predictable arc you'll follow as you move from inaction to action and start to make progress. Everyone I've ever coached starts off with some hesitation and uncertainty, then becomes intimidated by the realization of the big goals they've set and the effort they'll have to exert to reach them. But once they hit their stride and find ways to stay disciplined, they surprise themselves. It's great to see. Fill out this Hero Worksheet to get yourself thinking in these terms:

HERO WORKSHEET	
Origin story (What adversity did you overcome to get where you are today?)	
Superpowers (What are the strengths or skills you gained from that adversity?)	
Adversity (Are you facing any currently?)	
Strategies (What will you do when tempted to quit?)	
Sidekicks (Who can help you when things get hard?)	

UNCOMFORTABLE TRUTH NO. 14

Those who quit usually quit early.

People don't generally quit difficult things at the end. They quit early in the process because adversity triggers fear and insecurity, leading them to doubt their abilities and question their capacity to overcome challenges. To them, quitting and making up a lame excuse is preferable to failing. Get past the 25 percent mark of whatever mountain you're trying to climb, past the point where you feel stupid, awkward, out of shape, whatever. If you can make it that far, you stand a better chance of finishing.

YOUR PERSPECTIVE IS YOUR SUPERPOWER

Embracing adversity now and leaning into what's hard changes you for the better. The more effort you put in—the more you surrender to the reality that for a while, what you're doing is going to suck—the less uncomfortable life will be when you get to the other side.

Training harder today means you'll be fitter sooner and enjoy better energy, health, and athletic performance. You'll look better in your clothes and feel more confident. Saving money instead of going on a spree, even if it means giving up things, means you'll have more money for retirement or that big purchase. You'll also have less debt, which means more freedom. Eating healthy today, even if it means giving up unhealthy foods you love, means you're likely to have healthier weight, blood pressure, and blood sugar in the future, which should mean better long-term health, confidence, and possibly a lower chance of developing a chronic illness. Grinding through the tough days of starting your business now means faster client acquisition, the ability to hire and grow your team, and hopefully financial freedom down the road.

But the biggest change I see in people, as their perspective on adversity shifts, is that they learn to *appreciate* the uncomfort, the hard times, and the things that test them. It's true. Negative, closed-minded people who have been through rough patches might not see that time as an advantage. Tough times become their default reasons they can't do something. But seeing adversity that way is a *choice*. You can choose to frame adversity as an opportunity to overcome fears, to grow, and to prove to yourself what you can do.

Right now, if you're facing the beginning of a hard road to a more fulfilling career, a stronger marriage, or a fitter body, you have the privilege of *choosing* adversity. Other times, you might not be so lucky. Adversity will find you in the form of a health problem, financial crisis, layoff, divorce, or who knows what else. If you choose to confront and overcome adversity today, you'll be stronger, better, and more prepared when adversity takes you by surprise.

There's one more advantage to adversity and challenge: *they keep you from getting bored*. Boredom is the fastest road to complacency. When you're regularly trying new things, varying your routine, and aggressively expanding your comfort zone, you might be scared shitless, but you won't be bored. Continually walking eyes open into fresh challenges keeps your mind working and your senses firing. You're awake, testing new muscles and formulating new strategies. It's a great way to stay on course.

When you do find yourself confronting something daunting—a workout, a relationship conversation, a meeting at work, and so on—try asking yourself these questions:

ADVERSITY QUESTIONS

1. What makes me nervous about the adversity I'm facing? Am I afraid I can't handle it, or is it something else?

2. Is my fear or doubt rational? Is there proof or data to back up my fear and doubt, or am I just projecting based on my emotions? Have I successfully navigated something like this in the past?
3. Will focusing on the reward be enough to get me past my apprehension, or do I need more help?
4. What kind of help do I need? Coaching? Mentoring? Technology? Accountability?
5. How will overcoming this make me better? Is there pain I can recycle? How will it make the lives of other people better?
6. How can I change my environment or my Sunday Setup to help me dive into adversity and get it done?

Whatever you do, don't let your powers go unused. With great power comes great responsibility. It's going to be uncomfortable either way. Choose to turn the adversity you've faced—and will continue to face—into your greatest advantage.

MOMENTUM BUILDERS

NOW: Complete your Hero Worksheet. Have fun with this, and allow yourself to step into the superhero version of yourself.

TODAY: What pain are you ready to recycle? What change or decision have you been telling yourself you can't make, when really you can't afford not to? Answer the Adversity Questions to gain some clarity. It's imperative that you keep going, so your adversity plan is important.

STOP RENEGOTIATING YOUR CONTRACTS

Meet Dana, a bright and ambitious graphic designer with dreams of starting her own agency. She often sat by the window with a cup of tea, sketching designs and mapping out business plans. Dana decided it was time she made a promise to herself: she would launch her agency by the time she turned thirty. But as the months ticked closer to her deadline, Dana found herself repeatedly renegotiating the terms of her promise.

Initially, her goal was clear and the deadline firm. However, each time a freelance project ran late or a personal obligation cropped up, Dana adjusted her timeline. "Just one more month," she would rationalize, or "I'll start after this project is off my plate and I have more time." These renegotiations became a pattern and started to become her "norm." The deadline shifted further and further into the future, and with each adjustment, her initial excitement waned and was replaced by a nagging sense of unease.

This cycle of making and breaking promises with herself not only stalled her progress but also began eroding her self-confidence. Each renegotiated contract was a reminder of her inconsistency, which fed both her limiting beliefs and feelings of impostor syndrome. Dana watched as peers, who had set similar goals but adhered to their self-imposed deadlines, began to succeed. They faced the same challenges and distractions, but somehow, they held fast to their commitments.

One evening an old friend from college, who had just celebrated the fifth anniversary of her own start-up, asked Dana how her business plans were coming along. The question was a gut punch. Dana realized that her constant delays and renegotiations had cost her nearly five years. She could have been celebrating milestones like her friend, but instead, she was caught in a vicious loop of postponed dreams and diluted ambitions.

This moment of clarity was painful but necessary. Dana understood that renegotiating her contracts with herself was not just a harmless delay but also a dangerous barrier to achieving her dreams. It led to a growing cycle of regret and what-ifs. Even scarier, Dana realized her constant renegotiating had spilled into way more areas of her life than just her agency dream. She realized that to avoid a lifetime of regret, she needed to stop this pattern of self-renegotiation and treat her personal promises with the same seriousness as a binding contract with a client.

I'm sure many of you relate to Dana's story. We all intend to honor our contracts with ourselves. No renegotiation. But we don't. This doesn't just happen with our big, long-term dreams either. This habit of breaking promises to ourselves is one we face every day. We set a goal and make a plan—say, to get in shape. "I'm going to get up at five every morning and work out," you say to yourself. That's you signing the contract, and in that moment you have every intention of honoring it. Then your alarm goes off, and you hit the snooze button.

Renegotiation number one. When you finally get up, you say, "Okay, crap, I'll work out in between calls during my lunch hour." Another renegotiation!

Lunch hour comes, and work is slammed. You say, "Shit, I've got too much going on. I'll work out after work." Renegotiation number three. Five o'clock comes, and you've got to stay and work late. Renegotiation number four: "I'll work out at eight o'clock tonight." Eight o'clock finally rolls around, and, ugh, you're too full from dinner and tired from work! Screw it, you'll just work out twice as hard tomorrow. Renegotiation number five. You go home and go to bed having renegotiated yourself into a zero day.

Are you wincing in recognition right now? Maybe even ducking your head and saying, "You got me, Brett"? I'll bet you are because we all do this. We all renegotiate our contracts because we want to avoid feeling guilty about not doing what we promised ourselves we would do. Nobody's perfect. But the people who seem to be able to stay on track and not deviate from the path to their goals are the people who rarely, if ever, renegotiate their contracts.

The trouble with renegotiating contracts is that we lie to ourselves. We're very, very good at finding wiggle room and loopholes in any contract. We say, "I'll get back on the horse tomorrow," but then we do the same thing. We say we are going to do something 100 percent for thirty straight days and then after a week are already negotiating back to 75 percent. We put off doing what we don't want to do on Wednesday, and then on Thursday, and then on Friday, until finally we say, "Forget it. I'll start fresh on Monday." Of course, Monday comes, and we do the same thing all over again. Just like in Dana's story, that's how weeks, months, and years go by with us not making any real progress or moving our lives forward.

CALLING BULLSHIT

Why do we lie to ourselves about keeping our promises and honoring our contracts? Research shows that part of the reason is so we can more effectively deceive other people. Apparently, if we can get ourselves to believe something first, we're better at convincing others to believe it too. So if you convince yourself that you really will quit your job "one of these days" and walk the path of the freelance entrepreneur—even if you never seem to do it—you can sell the lie to other people, who then tell you how brave you are, how much they wish they were like you, and so on. It's a nice ego boost. Of course, the problem with this reality distortion is that it doesn't get you anywhere. Unless you quit renegotiating and act, you're still stuck in the same job. The solution? Stop lying to everyone, which is really just another way of lying to yourself.

THE SIGN NOW, PAY LATER CONUNDRUM

Here's where we get messed up. You need to do certain things now—work out, stop drinking, therapy with your spouse, take that sales seminar—to enjoy the benefits tomorrow. No sweat, right? Wrong. Because human beings are really bad at projecting outcomes into the future. We're wired to do what we want right now and worry about the future when it comes, even when we know we should give up some comfort or pleasure today to benefit a year from now. That's why, according to the Survey of Consumer Finances, almost half of American households had no retirement savings in 2022.* We suck at sacrificing now for the good of our future selves.

This "Sign now, pay later" conundrum is at the heart of our habit of signing contracts to get what we want without having to fork over any of the cash, effort, or sacrifice. Credit cards, student loans, car leases—they have taught us that we don't need to pay the piper until tomorrow, next

* Board of Governors of the Federal Reserve System. "Federal Reserve Board–Survey of Consumer Finances (SCF)." 2022. https://www.federalreserve.gov/econres/scfindex.htm.

month, or some point down the road. That's why we constantly renegotiate contracts with ourselves. Promises cost nothing. When it comes time to pay up, that's when we say, "Well . . . maybe not today." Without consequences, we'll always choose procrastination and ease.

In an interview the late legend Kobe Bryant talked about his famous, hypercompetitive "Mamba Mentality": "I'm not negotiating with myself," he said. "The deal was already made. I signed that contract and shook hands with myself, that is the deal, I'm doing it. Throughout that process you'll start talking to yourself like, *Man I gotta, I think I need to, maybe if we* . . . NOPE! Once you make that deal with yourself, there's no going back. This is nonnegotiable."*

You're not Kobe Bryant, and neither am I. His will was one of a kind. But how can mere mortals like us learn from his mentality and get past our constant self-sabotage and renegotiation? One way is to *stop signing so many contracts*. Most people, in a hurry to make change happen now, sign way too many contracts and commit to way too much. You're thinking, "I'm going to be great with food, get eight hours of sleep, and work out six days a week." Then life happens. You work out four days a week, feel like a failure, and drop every last ball you were juggling.

Commit to fewer things. Sign fewer contracts, and sign them in areas you're confident you can dominate and follow through. Let's say your goals revolve around getting your financial life in order: repairing your poor credit, paying off credit card debt, building up some emergency savings, and saving up a down payment for a house. Great. Now if you're in financial trouble because you have a problem with spending money and not paying your bills on time, those are the two areas where you should be signing contracts. Until you get your spending under control and fix your credit, you're not going to

---

* Goalcast. "His Secrets to Achieving Greatness | Kobe Bryant Speech." YouTube. March 3, 2020. https://www.youtube.com/watch?v=yyREZmeKvW0.

have money to save, and you're not going to get a mortgage, so what's the point in committing to do those things all at the same time?

Instead, what about putting yourself on a budget and setting a lower limit on your credit card? Starting with something manageable is the best way to build confidence in your ability to uphold the contracts you sign. Then after holding up your end of the bargain and proving it to yourself, move to putting some of your bills on bill pay and maybe even working with a legitimate debt consolidation service to lower your payments. Those are things you're confident you can do and see results.

When you succeed, you'll start feeling more confident because you're following through. You're starting to rack up wins and see results, which makes you more likely to honor future contracts. You don't want to give back the progress you've made.

SIMPLE BUT NOT EASY

Here's my advice: When you're looking at contracts to sign, focus on one personal thing and one professional thing. If you can handle more, you'll know it later, but right now, just rack up follow-through wins and build confidence that you can trust yourself. This is what I call "simple, not easy." Narrowing down to those few contracts where you can find success is a simple solution, but it's not easy to do. "Stop renegotiating your contracts" sounds easy, but if it was, millions of people wouldn't be so frustrated and discouraged. However, the ROI for following through is big.

One way to get past the "simple but not easy" barrier is to honor all the small contracts you've already signed. How about the small contract you made to start drinking more water? The contract of not hitting snooze when your alarm goes off? The contract of going to the morning class and not punting to a plan B afternoon class that may or may not happen? The contract of not sneaking cookies before dinner each night?

Those contracts might seem easy to honor, but that's because they're just a regular part of your life. But not honoring them is a slippery slope.

Nobody gets killed because you sneaked a few cookies before dinner, but that's still breaking your word to yourself, and that kills your confidence and trust in yourself. Until you connect the dots between these small failed promises and the damage to your integrity, you're going to remain in this confidence-killing cycle. Honoring those contracts reminds you that you *can* keep a commitment and do what's not easy.

UNCOMFORTABLE TRUTH NO. 15

The quickest way to kill your confidence is by signing bullshit contracts with yourself.

Don't sign contracts you know you won't honor. We all do it. We promise that we'll do something while knowing damn well when the moment of truth rolls around, we'll renegotiate. But that's crazy, isn't it? Why do we do that knowing it's keeping us stuck in Excuseville? Because we want the temporary self-esteem boost of committing to something healthy and empowering, we ignore that nagging inner voice that says, "Come on, you're not going to go to the gym six days next week! You've never done that before. Do you expect anyone to take this seriously?" Getting over this terrible habit is one of the most important steps you can take in becoming more disciplined. Discipline isn't just about the action you take; it's also about not lying to yourself about what you will or won't do in the future. Be honest with yourself. Brutally honest. Don't sign contracts you know you won't fulfill. Commit to things you're confident you'll do, the same way you would if you were committing to a close friend. As you stack proof that you can keep your commitments, it'll get easier to do harder things.

YOU'VE GOTTEN TOO GOOD AT LYING TO YOURSELF

The truth about renegotiation is that you're lying to yourself and locking yourself into a pattern of endless losing because it's too easy. There's no cost and no consequences. If you can find a way to create a consequence for yourself when you put off a commitment, great. If you can't, start thinking about renegotiation as what it is: *planning to lose.* That idea alone, that you're setting yourself up to lose again and again and again, might just be uncomfortable enough to break this cycle of lying to yourself.

In case that's not enough, here are three more ways to prevent contract renegotiation:

1. **Don't sign conflicting contracts.** Suppose one of your contracts is to lose weight so you can be healthier and have better mobility. Great. Unfortunately, one of your other contracts is to do more professional networking, and that often means going to events where there's a lot of fattening food and alcohol. Upholding the second contract will undermine your first one. Is your contract to advance at work forcing you to work more hours, sabotaging your other contract to spend more time with your kids? Don't stay in conflicting contracts. All your contracts must align and support each other. If they don't, drop the one that's least important to you.
2. **Protect your contract at all costs.** You must get better at saying no. If I ask you to lunch and you know that going to lunch is going to prevent you from doing something that will honor one of your contracts, then get comfortable with telling me no. You will never get better at keeping your word to yourself unless you get more

comfortable letting other people down. If your contract isn't something you'll fight to protect, you'll break it nine times out of ten. By the way, you're under no obligation to explain why you're saying no to something to protect your contract. If somebody doesn't understand why going to your son's ball game is more important than going to happy hour, that's their problem. Be strong and confident with your no's.

3. **Just start.** Getting started is always the hardest thing, whether we're talking about the day's exercise or filling out a job application. So if you're wavering and tempted to renegotiate, just start. Do the first five minutes of your workout or fill out the first three lines of the application. Become an object in motion. Odds are, once you get going, you'll keep going.

TAKE THE NEXT STEP NOW

Another way to prevent yourself from renegotiating is to shorten the time between making decisions and taking action. I view progress like two legs walking forward. Once you make a decision, that's like moving your right to take a step forward. To move your left foot forward, you need to take action. To prevent yourself from going in circles, you have to continue to make decisions *and* follow up with action. Then make another good decision, then more action. Now you're moving forward!

The quicker you make decisions and follow them with action, the faster you will pick up speed. Some people seem like they are practically *running* toward their goals, right? It's because they make quick decisions and take immediate action. They don't waste time, which allows them to make progress faster.

One final way people fall into the trap of *losing* is by taking too long to make important decisions. They waffle back and forth and are so concerned with making the perfect choice that they take forever to make any decision—and, sometimes, don't make one at all. These are my overthinkers, my fence sitters.

People often describe this by saying they feel "stuck." If that's a feeling you have right now, I want to challenge you:

Are you stuck, or are you just unwilling to make a bold decision?

Some of you reading this have been sitting too long on a decision that needs to be made. Many times, stress and anxiety around a situation arise not because you don't know what to do. It's due to knowing you are delaying and procrastinating on making a bold decision. You will struggle to play at your highest level and make progress if you can't make QDC: Quality Decisions Quickly. Instead of stressing over making the *right* decision, focus on making the best quick decision you can, and then immediately follow that with the right action. This will have you *sprinting* toward your goals in no time.

MOMENTUM BUILDERS

NOW: Write down all your current contracts and promises, all the things you're committed to. Now highlight the ones you continually keep renegotiating.

TODAY: Look at your list of current contracts. Get rid of every contract that you aren't positive you can keep your promise on. Are any of these contracts conflicting? If so, choose the most important one and drop the other. Do you need to tell someone "No," you cannot do something? Tell them right now. Use this as an opportunity to establish and recommit to only the contracts you are willing to sign with complete confidence. Just like goals, don't be afraid to start out by only signing smaller, short-term contracts with yourself that you know you can keep before you work your way up to bigger and longer-term ones.

WAKE UP!

I used to have a problem. It involved hitting the snooze button in the morning. Most of the truly fit, successful, and driven people I know don't hit the snooze button. They get up, get dressed, and get out the door. That's their autopilot response. Usually because they are excited for their day and for their life. They follow their plan whether they wake up feeling inspired and motivated or sluggish and lazy.

It's easy to get moving when you feel motivated and inspired. But another secret to success is:

Don't ask yourself questions that you don't want the answers to.

Asking yourself—if you are feeling motived or feel like doing something—is a bright shiny off-ramp begging you to renegotiate your commitment. Nothing will ever feel more comfortable than your warm, cozy bed in the morning. It really doesn't matter if it's 10:00 a.m. or 5:00 a.m. Waking up will never be a more comfortable decision than staying in bed. This is why you can't rely on allowing *how you feel* to dictate if you wake up or snooze.

Then one day I had a light bulb moment. I heard someone speaking about the promises and commitments we make to ourselves. I thought about my battle with the snooze button, and for the first time, it occurred to me that it wasn't just about me not wanting to get out of bed—it was me breaking the very first promise and commitment I made to myself that day. Not only did that sting; it also completely changed the way I viewed the snooze button from that moment on.

Once I retrained myself to conquer the snooze button, I realized that there are metaphorical snooze buttons scattered all over our lives. I was one of those people. I thought I would never be a "morning person"—that it was something you were born with. Of course, that's nonsense. Those statements about myself weren't facts; they were simply limiting beliefs that I continued to repeat. Taking control of my morning was the first step down a long and winding road that made me realize I could take control of everything that was holding me back from the life I wanted and felt I was capable of.

The snooze button is both a real thing and a metaphor for something much bigger. Any time you renegotiate your contract with yourself, it's the equivalent of hitting the snooze button. Whenever you decide you'd rather stay where you are rather than get uncomfortable, get moving, and make things happen, you're hitting the snooze button. It's different from the "Fuck It" button because you're not giving up; you're selling yourself the story that in a few minutes, you'll get up and get back to your plan. But most of the time, when the alarm buzzes, you smash the button again.

Just like Dana "snoozing" the start of her business, you can snooze your life away. You know how you keep hitting the snooze button while you're half asleep and then wake up in a panic because you're late for work? You can keep hitting the snooze button on your change plan, and suddenly, ten years have gone by, and you've changed nothing. It's like you're living the movie *Groundhog Day*!

For me, the snooze button became a microcosm of all the shit I was complaining about but doing nothing about. It was not about ten more minutes of sleep. It was about mistaking *intention* for *action*. I had good intentions, so everything would be fine. One of these days, I would get moving and really change things. But intentions don't mean much and never move the needle. All of a sudden, I started hitting the snooze button all over my life, putting off what I knew I had to do.

I had no idea how much that was hurting my life. Everything started to change when I made the unbreakable commitment that no matter what, I would get out of bed and start my day on time. I would get a win under my belt immediately. The days of starting my day down 0–1 were over. This was a helpful and obvious addition to my "Never Miss a Monday" mantra: *never hit snooze on Monday*. That eventually became an everyday habit.

"Wake up" is also a reminder that you're not immortal. You don't have unlimited time to finally get around to making your life what you want it to be. Time is the number one thing we take for granted until late in life when, sadly, it's the only thing that matters. If you don't want to be a cautionary tale and if you don't want to be filled with regret over what you might have done, in your twenties, thirties, forties, fifties, and so on, the first thing to do is wake up, turn off the alarm, and log a win while the unambitious stay asleep dreaming.

CALLING BULLSHIT

At the very least, the snooze button is an effective way to steal a few more minutes of extra rest, right? Wrong! Sleep specialists agree that these additional few minutes are far from restorative. When you hit snooze and fall back asleep, you're likely entering a new sleep cycle that you won't be able to complete, leading to you feeling more tired than if you had just gotten up with your first alarm. This is due to something called "sleep inertia," the grogginess you feel upon waking, which can be intensified by repeatedly interrupting your sleep cycle. It's better to set your alarm for when you actually need to get up and allow your body to wake up only one time.

SNOOZE BUTTONS ARE EVERYWHERE

There are snooze buttons all over our lives. Anywhere there's a contract, there's a snooze button. Here are some examples:

- The obvious one, not getting out of bed on time.
- Skipping the morning workout like you planned and opting for after work.
- Saying you'll fast until noon and then scarfing a donut that someone brought into the office that morning.
- Pushing off that tough conversation with your spouse and allowing resentment to build.
- Committing to Sober October and then realizing your friend's birthday is that month, so you give yourself a pass that weekend . . . and also Halloween weekend.
- Knowing you should repair your relationship with your mom or dad before something happens and it's too late, but you refuse to pick up the phone and call.

Every time one of those commitments comes up and you say, "Not this time, next time," you're renegotiating that contract and breaking a promise to yourself. You're lying to yourself, too, saying that there will always be another chance and that one day you'll get it right. But eventually, you run out of chances. You get sick. Your partner leaves. Your parents pass. The promotion you wanted goes to someone else. You get too old to take the trip or hike the epic mountain.

Hitting the snooze button is also a surefire way to kill your momentum. If I lose the first ten minutes of my day, I'm probably going to lose the first thirty minutes. It snowballs. But the dangerous part is that hitting the snooze button on your day soon becomes hitting the snooze button on your entire life.

Do you know someone who's said for years how they were going to take a big trip, invent a product, or run a marathon? But they never did those things, did they? That person hit life's snooze button over and over until life took choices away from them. They had kids. They had a mortgage. Their parents went into a nursing home. The next thing they knew, their knees hurt, and they couldn't do those things anymore.

This is not an exaggeration or a scare tactic. It's real. Time passes faster than you think, and we all think we have more time than we actually do. There are millions of people who have hit too many snooze buttons and can never go back to the lives they once envisioned. They've snoozed themselves into regret over all the great things left undone.

Unfortunately, my dad was one of those people. He always dreamed of living by the beach and being able to wake up and take a walk by the ocean (as shown on the next page) every day but figured he would wait until he retired to make that happen. It was a dream he was fully convinced would be available for him down the road. So he continually snoozed, and, unfortunately, he never got the chance.

Around the age of thirty, I realized I was heading down this same path in a cycle of renegotiations, convincing myself that all my dreams would still be available later. That was a huge motivator for me to stop snoozing. It's why I took the leap to start working for myself and why I moved to San Diego for two years and then to Florida. I saw firsthand how big the regret could be, and I wasn't willing to delay gratification any longer. I've never been happier living in warm weather near the ocean. Accomplishing that dream felt like it was for me—and for my dad.

Do you want to prevent a life of regret? Conquer the snooze button. Instead of thinking you have unlimited time, resources, and freedom, think in terms of making your mornings count. Get up, get out, get moving, and don't assume there will always be time.

Write down some things in the chart that follows that you keep hitting the snooze button on and how long you've been doing it. For example, "Putting off seeing a therapist" and "Six years":

SNOOZE BUTTON	HOW LONG?

Were you shocked by what and for how long you've been breaking the contract with yourself over something that's pretty important, such as going back to school, getting your eating under control, or dealing with a history of trauma? Good. Now your eyes are open, and you know what to do.

UNCOMFORTABLE TRUTH NO. 16

You're scared, and that's okay.

Attaching conditions to the things you want to do is what I call "backdoor cowardice." Wait, what? Backdoor cowardice is when you don't want to admit you're afraid, so you set yourself up so that you won't have to face your fear. Your job's been stealing your joy for years, so you say, "I'll look for a new job as soon as I get promoted to VP." But once that happens you'll get a pay raise, and be twice as busy, which will make it that much harder to leave. You're just giving yourself an out in the same way you say, "I'll make my trek on the Camino de Santiago once I learn to speak fluent Spanish." But you know you'll never do that, so you never have to face traveling to a strange place where you don't speak the language. Does this sound familiar? If you're going to set conditions for doing things, make them short term and realistic. Otherwise, you're just telling yourself one more lie and giving yourself too much wiggle room to snooze and renegotiate.

EARLY MOMENTUM

I've also noticed that fulfilled individuals are universally grateful for the things in their life that they didn't delay. They all took the risk and bet on themselves instead of letting fear force them into another snooze. They realize that you never know when something could happen that will change your life for the better, and they also know that opportunities like that are a lot less likely to happen if you're sleeping through life.

People see me now, a guy who rarely drinks, is fit, and has his own business, and they'll say, "Brett, so you never drank?" And I'll tell them that I drank a lifetime's worth in my twenties and did it at a professional level. Would it have been nice to get this whole business thing started sooner? Sure, but that wasn't my biggest goal at that time. Fun and experiences were. I have zero regrets about how I spent my twenties. I'm so glad I took a trip to Cabo San Lucas with my cousin and one of my best friends when I was twenty-seven because it was one of the most fun trips of my life. It was epic in every way. That trip wouldn't be the same now. Sure it would be fun, but we wouldn't be drinking margaritas for breakfast and dancing on tables with locals.

When I was starting my business and watching all those motivational videos every morning, I realized most of the greats started their day early. Most get more done before noon than the average person does all day. Why? Because winning their morning is nonnegotiable. They wake up with purpose and a plan. Mornings are the best because you have fewer distractions. Everybody else is asleep. The phone's not ringing. Emails aren't flooding in yet. It's your time. You can set the tone for your day. You can accomplish something immediately and gain some early momentum.

Win your morning. Get up and do one impactful thing for yourself that will have a positive ripple effect on your day. Maybe for you, that's drinking your water and meditating for fifteen minutes. For someone else, it might mean writing in your journal and getting some work done on your business plan. For the busy parent, even waking up twenty minutes before your kids gives you a few moments of peaceful quiet time before the chaos of the day begins. It doesn't matter. What matters is that you make a solemn promise to yourself that morning is *your* time. It's your first promise of the day, and it sets the tone for the day. If you break it, you'll be *pissed* at yourself.

Here are some effective ways I've found to beat the snooze and win your morning:

1. **Know what you're getting up for.** Determine exactly what you're going to do for those first thirty minutes: get dressed, make coffee, eat breakfast, read the *New York Times*, whatever. It's easier not to hit snooze if you're excited about getting up. If you use your morning time for something you really enjoy, you'll *want* to wake up for that.
2. **Set your alarm for the time you have to get up.** Don't set it for forty minutes earlier. Set the alarm for the time that you actually have to wake up so you're not running behind. Remember, our brains are master negotiators. If we can invent plan B and plan C to wiggle out of a commitment, we'll do it. Especially when those negotiations are coming from the warm confines of our bed. Don't give yourself the option. This is also a smart way to get more quality sleep than wasting that snooze time dragging yourself in and out of consciousness, which is scientifically proven to add grogginess to your morning.

3. **Change your alarm ringtone.** Right now, your brain is programmed to hear that familiar noise and hit snooze as quickly as possible. You need to rewire that autopilot response. Changing your alarm ringtone is the best way to create an unfamiliar sound and override your brain's normal response system. That will have your brain asking, "What is that?" That could be all you need to retrain yourself: you changed that tone for a reason, and hitting snooze is no longer an option! When I was breaking this habit, I changed my alarm to "Circle of Life" from *The Lion King*. No, I'm not kidding. What started as a sarcastic joke actually made me smile, and feel inspired every morning I heard it. I imagined Simba looking up to the dark sky and receiving the wakeup call from the vision of his dad, Mufasa: "Look inside yourself. You are more than what you have become." That ringtone was the uncomfortable reminder I needed that I chose that sound for a reason. That it was time to wake up, win my morning, and start living up to my potential.
4. **Have everything set up and ready.** From your workout clothes and shoes to the foods you need to make breakfast, have it all in place and easy to grab. Reduce as much friction as you can between you and the great morning you want to have.

LIFE WON'T WAIT FOR YOU

The other part of "waking up" is realizing that life doesn't give a shit about your milestones. It's not going to wait for you. Father Time is undefeated, and weeks and months will pass regardless of whether you utilize that time or not. It's not going to wait for the perfect time. It's not going to wait for you to be comfortable traveling to a country where you don't speak the language or going to a venture capital firm and pitching them to give you seed capital. So then why are you qualifying your happiness?

Qualifying your happiness looks like this: "I'll quit my job when I have $10,000 saved." "I'll go on my dream trip once things slow down at work." "I'll leave him if he cheats one more time." "I'll patch things up with Dad when the kids get older."

Yeah, sure you will.

Why are you putting conditions on the things that will make you happier? When you do that, you're creating wiggle room to renegotiate your contract. There's always a reason not to do something uncomfortable, and the more conditions added, the more likely you are to back out.

Instead, find the goals you're passionate about and say, "I'm going to quit my job" or "I'm going to relocate to a new city." Bury the rest of the sentence. When you know, you know. Now figure out what you need to do each morning to make that happen and get to work, knowing there's no amount of work or prep you can do that will make taking that leap less uncomfortable. It will be disorienting and unnerving, and maybe even expensive. But you'll be taking a big leap and honoring your contract with yourself.

MOMENTUM BUILDERS

NOW: Complete your personal snooze button list. What one step can you take immediately in each area you've been snoozing, and how can you make sure that step happens by the end of the day?

TODAY: Change your ringtone to something that fires you up, makes you smile, or makes waking up a moment of truth by programming motivational messages to appear on your home screen when you get up. This will rewire your brain from default snooze to a deliberate and conscious choice to get out of bed and make the day matter.

PART V

EXPECT IT TO BE HARD

PLAY THE LONG GAME WITH PATIENCE AND THE SHORT GAME WITH URGENCY

Shortly after I moved from Northern Virginia to San Diego, adversity struck again when the long-term relationship I was in ended abruptly. While I knew deep down it needed to happen, it shook my world. Here I was, across the country from all my friends and family, in a brand-new city, about to move for the third time in two years, and feeling like I was starting over—again.

I was a mess, and for a while it felt like everything in my life had gotten "hard." Dragging myself to the gym, cooking dinner, or even showing up for a coaching call felt impossible. I was in a funk, and something needed to change. It was at that time that a former client mentioned a marathon ruck coming up back in the DC area. A *ruck* is a long-distance walk, jog, or hike while wearing a weighted pack or vest. I previously mentioned my little interest in running a marathon because I didn't enjoy running. But with how crappy I was already feeling, the idea of having to wear a twenty-five-pound weighted vest for 26.2 freakin' miles now sounded intriguing. It sounded so incredibly hard and uncomfortable that somehow it was attractive to me. I was also scared shitless. "What if I fail? What if I can't do it? What if I get hurt? What if this doesn't work and doesn't make me feel any better?" I heard all the fears, but some little voice kept telling me, "I need to do this."

Training for this ruck would be the perfect way for me to *raise my hard ceiling*, a phrase I actually coined out on the long, lonely miles training for those rucks. Because of how many hours and how much sweat went into training for this race, everything else in my life began to feel easier by comparison. If I could go out and ruck eight miles before 8:00 a.m., how could anything else in my day seem hard after that? That changed everything for me. Flying back to DC wasn't an option due to moving into my new apartment the same week, but I forced myself to keep the race date as my deadline so that I couldn't negotiate my way out of it. So less than eight weeks later, without any other racers, a single fan cheering, or volunteers handing out water, I completed my first marathon, completely solo and wearing that weighted vest. It took me just over seven hours. My hard ceiling hadn't just been raised; it had been obliterated. The idea of moving into a new place and rebuilding my life suddenly seemed easier, and because I took bold action, my confidence was returning as well.

Sometimes, things feel hard because you've allowed your *hard ceiling* to get too low. While I agree that completing a marathon in eight weeks with a weighted vest is pretty extreme and not something I recommend, there is indescribable value in raising your hard ceiling. This is why most entrepreneurs, endurance athletes, and high performers don't get tripped up by the small, mundane tasks. They don't seem hard compared with the bigger tasks they've already tackled. If you've worked twenty-hour days to raise money and get a start-up off the ground, working late one weekend on a PowerPoint deck is a piece of cake.

The higher your *hard ceiling* becomes, the more you expand your comfort zone and the easier it becomes to overcome the little uncomforts life will throw at you.

"HOW LONG?" IS THE WRONG QUESTION

If somebody asked me, "Brett, how long does it take to get from Florida to New York?" before I could give them an accurate answer, I'd need to ask some additional questions. How are you getting there? Are you riding your bike? Are you driving? Are you flying? Depending on how you're traveling, I'll give you a very different answer.

Throughout my career, the most common question I've heard from people is, "Brett, how long will it take me to ______?" You can fill in that blank with any goal they may have. How long until they have a fit body, master a new skill, have a certain amount of money saved, get our employees to buy into our new company vision, get to one hundred thousand subscribers on YouTube, get to $5 million with their business, and so on? They're expecting me to provide a time-based answer, and you might be too. But here's why that's my least favorite question and, more importantly, the wrong question.

First, it's wrong because no two people will have the same experience in trying to reach a goal. Even if their circumstances are identical (which they never are), they're going to travel a different path. Take two individuals with the same goal of getting down to 15 percent body fat. They both commit to 120 hours of workouts, but one of them finishes those 120 hours in six months, while the other one takes a year to complete the same number of workout hours. The first person will almost certainly reach the 15 percent goal sooner than the second person because they've compressed the work into a shorter amount of time. The secret to their success isn't the amount of time because both people exercised for 120 hours. It's the reps that the first person put in within that time.

The second reason "How long?" is the wrong question is because time, by itself, changes absolutely nothing. If you give yourself five years to build a $1 million stock portfolio but during that time you don't invest any money in stocks, at the end of five years, the only thing you are is older. Time only matters when you use that time to execute the reps that will eventually deliver the results. You work out at the gym. You make regular credit card payments. You practice the guitar. You execute the company vision on a day in and day out basis. When you fill time with quality reps, you get results. But it's the effort and new habits that drive the results, not the time.

The Beatles didn't magically emerge overnight. They played about twelve hundred live shows between 1960 and 1964 in bars and clubs in places such as Liverpool and Hamburg, Germany. Most bands don't play that many shows over decades. They were putting in their quality reps, their ten thousand hours. Those intense and consistent habits sharpened their playing, singing, and writing until they were the best band on the planet.

CALLING BULLSHIT

Extreme self-improvement regimens such as 75 Hard and Whole30 have gained a following because they promise to help you change your habits over a short time. Can some people get through them and see results? Absolutely. Trouble is, habits don't change through sheer force of will, so the changes people experience rarely last. Most people either fail and quit due to the all-or-nothing approach or finish their seventy-five days and then struggle to maintain any of the momentum they've gained. I understand why people are attracted to programs and challenges such as this, because going all in feels like the fastest way to make a big change. This is the classic case of intensity over consistency and why quality reps, not shortest time, should be your target. Stop worrying about intensity, and set your aim on consistency. Consistency will help you win both the short and the long game.

KEEP "MOVING THE CHAINS"

As you progress toward your goals, you'll get more mileage out of focusing your attention on getting in your reps than you will out of worrying about the time it takes to reach the finish line. It's normal to want to set a time frame for goals. You want to drop twenty pounds by your class reunion or your wedding. You want to have a great new job by the time you turn thirty. I get it. But you can't control time. You *can* control your effort and consistency.

Life happens. You get injured, a parent gets sick, or you just get buried at work, and all of a sudden, your carefully crafted timeline is wishful thinking. But energy, effort, and commitment are all in your control. If you're focused on reps, you can easily speed up or slow down depending on your schedule and energy level. Remember the work we did on perfectionism? You can slow down and still remain consistent. That's why focusing on reps is magic. If your motto becomes "Just get it done," and you're all about knocking out those reps because doing that is nonnegotiable, you're going to get the results you want faster.

This is about *prioritizing effort over outcome.* You can't snap your fingers and have the outcome you want because life doesn't work that way. What you can do is put consistent effort into the activities you know will eventually get you to your goal, whether it's losing twenty pounds or paying off your massive credit card bill. You can work out five days a week and eat a clean, lean diet. You can cut up your credit cards and make a nonminimum payment on time every month. Do that, keep your head down, and, inevitably, you will get that outcome.

My advice to anyone looking to accomplish a big goal or make a massive change in their life is to *expect it to be hard.* On the surface, this may seem discouraging, but it may be the most valuable mindset shift you can adopt. When you expect something to be easy, sooner or later you will be smacked in the face with a challenge, a setback, or a test to see how badly you really want it. If you're mentally unprepared to face an obstacle, you'll stumble, second-guess yourself, or quit. If you expect to do anything great or impactful with your life, expect it to get hard at some point. That's what makes it worth it.

Anyone can keep going when it's easy, but if you expect it to be hard, you'll plan for hard, and when the hard eventually shows up, which it will, you'll be ready for it.

Resist the urge to try for a touchdown on every play. Instead, keep "moving the chains" each week and focus on making first down after first down. I know, you want results fast, but this mentality causes people to look for every shortcut and to throw Hail Mary passes instead of trusting momentum and consistency to move forward. First downs lead to touchdowns, and it's a lot easier to score from the one-yard line than it is from midfield. Trust your effort, and before you know it you'll be standing in the end zone celebrating!

So no more asking, "How long will it take to get in shape?" Instead, say, "I'm going to get in six miles of walking five days a week." Instead of asking, "How many social media posts will it take for me to gain ten thousand followers?" say, "I'm going to put up five engaging Instagram posts a week like clockwork." Let that be your discipline, and let the results take care of themselves—because in the end, *that's all you can control.*

UNCOMFORTABLE TRUTH NO. 17

Your goal will take longer than you want.

What you want will almost always take longer to achieve than you tell yourself. Why? First, we tend to delude ourselves about our discipline, especially in the beginning of a program of change. We vow to eat our Tupperware breakfast . . . until somebody brings bagels to the office. Second, being consistent from week to week will take time and practice, even if you do your Sunday Setup. The demands on your time can vary wildly, and that means meditating or going after new customers for your small business might get pushed back. Third, some stuff worth having just takes time. The pace of weight loss varies from person to person. Interest can slow your debt payoff. Building your social media following depends on all kinds of factors, from algorithms to trends to learning what your audience considers valuable. This is why it's important to be patient.

ONE LONG GAME MADE UP OF A LOT OF SHORT GAMES

Of course, the wild card here is results, right? You want results. You're aching to see them, and it's ridiculous for me to tell you not to look at the scale or your bank account because you're going to. Truthfully, there is some value in looking at your results. Numbers don't lie, and for many people they're the greatest form of accountability. If you've made progress, you'll be encouraged and motivated to stay disciplined. The trouble comes when results are slow to arrive, and that messes with your head, or when chasing results interferes with your consistency because you take shortcuts. For instance, if you become obsessed with losing five more pounds in the last week before your high school reunion and you start skipping meals, that's a backward step for your overall health.

Here's my advice about checking out your results:

Play the long game with patience
and the short game with urgency.

Over the course of a year, I'm sure you want to do a lot of winning. But those wins will happen over the course of a lot of short games. That's why I prefer to stay focused on ninety-day windows, or less. Winning those short games means acting deliberately and with urgency during those days and weeks, making effort the goal, not outcomes. Prioritize getting in your reps at the gym or in your studies for your master's degree. Don't let anyone compromise the time you've set aside for meditation, seeing a therapist, or acting on the IPAs (income-producing activities) for your small business.

All the while, be patient and kind to yourself, confident that as long as you act with urgency and get your reps consistently, the results will come. Consistent high effort yields positive results 100 percent of the time. It *always* works. Will the results be exactly what you had in mind? Maybe. Will they appear exactly when you want? Probably not; results are not Amazon Prime. But you *will* get results.

SMALL WINS ADD UP

Every *outcome* goal is a result of reaching a long series of *effort* goals. If your effort goal is to walk twenty-five miles per week and you hit or beat that goal, I'm giving you a high five no matter what the scale says because you nailed the part you have full control over. So it's critical that you treat your reps as part of your results—and give yourself credit for those results.

Take pride in getting in your reps, and you'll feel better, build more momentum, and gain more confidence. Give yourself a high five for doing what's hard. I want you to feel good about hitting your effort goal every week. If you meet your effort goal and take pride in it, you'll feel more inspired and more confident the next week. When you hear people say, "Trust the process," this is what they mean. Focus on your effort and trust that it will lead you where you want to go.

Reps equal momentum. But I can't sit here and tell you that time isn't part of the equation at all because it is. You only have so much time, and you need to see results sooner or later. That's human nature. That's why it's also important to celebrate small wins. I'd rather you not fixate on the scale or your bank account, but instead, set some incremental milestones such as the following:

- Complete twenty workouts in a month.
- Meditate for five minutes a day.
- Boost your credit by making all payments on time for ninety days.
- Stay under your one-hour screen time limit on social media.
- Finish a book you've been reading (like this one).

Every time you knock off one of those milestones, throw yourself a little party. Just make sure your celebration doesn't hinder your progress toward your big goal (i.e., don't reward yourself for a week of great eating by bingeing at the buffet). Small celebrations and touchdown dances keep your spirits up and make it easier to keep your attention on getting your reps and putting in the effort.

In the end, effort > results. Consistently putting in the effort changes you and does amazing things to your self-worth and confidence. Over time, it turns you into a more focused, patient, disciplined, relentless version of yourself. Over time, the mindset of obsessing over reps, not results, will make you unstoppable.

MOMENTUM BUILDERS

NOW: List two areas or goals where you've been more focused on time and results, instead of effort. Now set a very specific effort-based goal for each of them. For example, you are patiently waiting for the end of the year to ask for a promotion. Instead, every two months, you schedule a meeting with your VP to assess your progress and opportunities for you to continue to grow and enhance your leadership skills.

TODAY: Commit to a certain number of reps you will complete this week and decide exactly what day and time rep one will take place.

CONSEQUENCES

I wanted to write a book like this one for years. I had the idea for so long that I had a running Google Doc titled *Future Book* that was jammed with potential topics, chapters, and unfinished thoughts. The date at the top of that doc? March 14, 2018.

Yikes. See, you and I are not so different. I messed around with the process, played with ideas and deadlines, and tried to make it happen, but I just couldn't get there by myself. Finally, I made another *big decision* and hired an editor to collaborate with me on writing the book, and I laid down significant cash for things such as design and marketing. You know what happened? The book you're holding in your hands (or listening to or scrolling on your phone) right now. It's also interesting to note that I felt the urge to first create that "future book" document in 2018, on my thirty-first birthday. Perhaps I was reflecting on the regret I would feel if I continued to snooze this goal of mine and never attempted to bring this book to life.

Spending money to write my book meant something was at stake. It gave me major skin in the game. I knew that once I paid people, if I still didn't follow through on writing the manuscript, that money would be gone, and I'd have nothing to show for it. Worse, it would be 100 percent my fault. Therefore, I followed through, got the book done, and here we are.

It's impossible to go toe-to-toe with uncomfort without a structure to hold yourself accountable. There have to be consequences for trying to renegotiate your contract or failing to show up and do what you're supposed to do. I've said that the most successful people in the world are the ones who find ways to get themselves to do what they don't want to do; one of those ways is by imposing consequences on themselves.

Whether you honor your contract or not, you're going to face consequences. If you embrace uncomfort and try to follow a plan and fail, you'll face consequences. Maybe you'll lose money or feel embarrassed. But that's better than the consequences you'll face if you do nothing, sitting in your recliner, watching your life go by, making plans and telling yourself that things will change one day. Those consequences will be brutal and, sometimes, permanent. There is nothing more heartbreaking than hearing an elderly person talk about the regrets they have about the things they never attempted or went after. Consequences—stakes, or skin in the game—are your fail-safe, making sure that the rest of the ideas I've shared in this book are workable. You need a meaningful accountability structure, and you need it from the start.

Accountability works, especially *external accountability*. We know that because in other areas of life, where it's imposed on us from the outside, it creates results. The most obvious example is work. You show up at your job and do the work because if you don't, you'll get fired. You probably also like receiving a paycheck. There are easily a half dozen crystal clear consequences for breaking your contract, and because of that, you don't break it. It doesn't matter if a consequence is internally or externally imposed or positive or negative. All that matters is that it compels you to do what you're supposed to do when you don't feel like doing it.

CALLING BULLSHIT

There's a school of thought that says the meaner, harsher, and more unforgiving you are with yourself, the better results you'll get from a change program. That's terrible advice. That's like being your own drill sergeant and screaming into your own face that you're a worthless loser. I had coaches like that growing up, and I never played my best for them. Don't get me wrong: I love me some David Goggins; I just don't think most of us are wired the same way he is. You might be tempted to berate yourself and call yourself names after you blow a diet or spend money you shouldn't have, but will that motivate you or help you make your next best decision? Most likely it will not. It's just going to trash your self-esteem, make you feel like a an imbecile, and make you more tempted to hit the "Fuck It" button. Remember, our brains listen to and believe our self-talk, which is why disempowering self-talk can be crippling and actually feed our limiting beliefs. If you mess up, own it, and then get back on the train as quickly as possible. This isn't an invitation to bullshit yourself or allow excuses to rule your life, but it's crucial to be both brutally honest *and* encouraging. Don't wait and feel bad. Act and feel better. That's how you turn things around.

THE SLOW DEATH OF INACTION

Human beings are lazy and enjoy comfort, which is why we need consequences to kick us in the ass every so often to keep moving. No matter how disciplined you think you are, you know the skeletons that lurk in your closet: all the dreams you've delayed, the goals you've said "One of these days" about. I'm the same way. The difference is that I've seen the consequences of inaction up close, both with my dad and with the conversations I've had with the Brett in the mirror.

For too long I was not living the life I knew deep down I was capable of, wasting precious time and being unhappy, and settling for the most complacent path. Just the memory of that time is enough of a consequence to get my ass moving even on those mornings when I'm tempted to rekindle my affair with the snooze button. But we don't all have that perspective. In fact, most human beings don't respond well to the prospect of long-term consequences for their choices. If they did, there wouldn't be so many millions of Americans eating garbage and becoming obese because they would take their doctors' warnings of diabetes and heart disease more seriously. A financial planner wagging his finger at you and saying, "If you don't save more money, you're never going to be able to retire," isn't going to make most thirty-year-olds suddenly start putting away one-fourth of their income. The time horizon of that consequence is too long to motivate us to change our spending habits and stop us from buying what we want today.

But being uncomfortable *now* does actually motivate us. If you look around your life, you can probably identify the areas where you feel embarrassed, unhappy, or desperate for change. If you sit around with friends talking about money and you feel anxious because you haven't looked in your bank account in a while and know you have no savings, that's an uncomfortable consequence of inaction. If you're trapped in an unhappy relationship because you won't fix it or get out, that's another uncomfortable consequence of inaction.

You're already experiencing the uncomfortable, slow death of knowing there are changes that need to be made but continuing to push them off. You don't have to manufacture immediate consequences; you're living them. Over and over, every single day. Now you just have to *act* on them.

MULTIPLE LAYERS

We inherently suck at holding ourselves accountable. We tend to choose negative consequences that are weak or that we can wiggle out of or renegotiate, or we choose rewards or incentives—stuff we like. But if you want to create accountability in your personal life, which you must do to feel successful, you'll have to accept an unpopular idea:

Holding yourself accountable usually means making yourself suffer.

Rewards sound great in theory. You keep your commitments and you get a cookie! But what you're really doing is staying in comfort. "I'm going to do this thing, and it's going to be magical and easy!" But you're feeding your own sense of comfort by thinking this yellow brick road will be easy to follow and that you won't have to battle the terrifying flying monkeys somewhere along the way. The trouble is, science shows us that when it comes to motivating action, rewards do not work as well as losses. Research by Nobel Prize–winning behavioral economist Daniel Kahneman found that in all kinds of situations, the pain of a loss is twice as powerful psychologically as the pleasure we get from a gain.*

This is why I say that real accountability means deliberately setting yourself up to suffer if you break your contract. Pain and fear are spectacular motivators because we don't like being hurt. As I mentioned earlier, when you work a 9–5, you show up for your job even when you don't want to because there are consequences if you don't. Yeah, your boss will fire you, and you won't be able to pay your mortgage, but you

* Kahneman, D., and A. Tversky. "Prospect Theory: An Analysis of Decision Making Under Risk." 1977. https://doi.org/10.21236/ada045771.

also might be held accountable by the thought of your colleagues, your customers, your spouse, and your kids. Multiple layers of external accountability are baked into your professional life but few, if any, in your personal life. It's not a coincidence that most people show more consistency at work than they do with their own health, goals, and dreams. The trick is to set up multiple layers of accountability anywhere you plan to make major changes in your life. These layers should be as follows:

- **A mix of consequences and rewards.** It's important to know that you'll suffer if you skip out on a commitment, but there have to be some encouraging incentives built in too.
- **Nonnegotiable and irreversible.** You shouldn't be able to back out of the painful stuff. An old client used to call this "unavoidable accountability," meaning there were multiple layers of accountability, as well as painful consequences, and zero chance of wiggling out of them or renegotiating.
- **Meaningful.** If your consequence causes you no pain, it has no power. If you're not a football fan, not getting to watch the game on Sunday because you skipped your workouts means nothing. Meaningful consequences cost you money, deny you something you want, embarrass you publicly, and so on. I know this seems harsh, but it's no different from the stakes that keep you making choices that prevent you from getting fired from your job.
- **Immediate.** As I said, we're bad at giving long-term consequences any real weight. Any reward or pain should happen quickly—immediately, if possible.

UNCOMFORTABLE TRUTH NO. 18

Friends, family, and significant others make terrible "account-abilibuddies."

Choosing a friend or your spouse as your "accountabilibuddy" (someone who holds you accountable) usually doesn't work out. That's because they care about you and will too often let you off the hook. It can even cause unwanted animosity on both sides when they are forced to be the "bad guy." When you're selecting people to hold you accountable, make sure they're people whom you really don't want to disappoint and who aren't afraid to kick your ass and piss you off—maybe someone you really look up to and would be embarrassed to let down. There's no right answer for everyone. Just don't assume that you *will* care about someone's opinion just because you *should*.

"ACCOUNTABILIBUDDIES"

Of course, the big question is: How do you enforce accountability on yourself? The short answer is, you don't. At least not early on. Instead, one of the resources I suggest you rely on is an accountability buddy, or "accountabilibuddy." That's somebody who's going to hold you accountable, not bullshit you, give it to you straight, and enforce consequences according to conditions you set.

This can be tricky. Finding someone who cares about you enough to hold your feet to the fire when you don't come through on your commitments is difficult. I'm talking about someone who will withhold concert tickets at your direction if you fail to send a picture from your phone of you working out that day. That's not easy to find because friends care about you. Friends and spouses want to see you happy, and they certainly don't want to be the ones to enforce your painful consequences. In fact, effective accountability buddies are so rare and hard to find that if you need a person to enforce consequences, consider hiring a personal coach.

That's not a sales pitch, but it is a reality. I'm not saying that you can't make big changes in your life on your own or that you can't impose your own consequences. I am saying that it's very difficult to do both. That's why almost every high achiever has some sort of mentor, performance coach, accountability group, or trainer. Sometimes, they have all four.

It's simple. We don't like to put ourselves through pain. That's why kids don't hold themselves accountable. Parents do. It's why puppies don't keep themselves accountable. Their owners do. An external source of accountability doesn't care about your short-term comfort, just your long-term results. Their priority is not to be your friend but to be your coach, so they don't mind kicking your ass. A great accountabilibuddy tells you what you *need* to hear, not what you *want* to hear.

It's not that I don't want you to build your internal accountability. I absolutely do. That's the key to long-lasting discipline, but that is not the most effective place to start. People who think they can make big changes with purely internal accountability usually fail. If you want to do this right, start with a blend of self-accountability and heavy external accountability.

Consider hiring help—a coach, trainer, business mentor, therapist, a personal CFO—someone with whom you can have straight, honest, zero-bullshit talks and who will work with you to set up your self-accountability and external accountability systems.

DEADLINES

A few years ago, I had a coach who knew how important fitness was to me. He also knew that writing my newsletter—at the time a new weekly commitment for me—was important to me. The problem was, I kept cramming the final bit of writing in on Saturday to ensure I could hit my Sunday morning distribution deadline. We both knew my best bet was to get it done on Mondays, but I couldn't seem to get that to stick consistently. So he told me, "Brett, you can't go to the gym on Mondays until you write your newsletter."

Well, I sure as hell didn't want to do that. As you know, Mondays and mornings are kinda my thing. I love working out on Monday morning. But he was firm. He said, "Nope, for the next month, you're not going on Monday until you write your newsletter." I hated that, but guess what? I wrote that newsletter at light speed Monday morning, and sometimes even Sunday night, because I hated not being able to work out first thing Monday morning. A good accountabilibuddy will be firm with you. You may hate them at times, but you still won't want to let them down.

That's accountability that's "sticky," meaning it works over and over again. If you get a paycheck every two weeks, that's two times a month you are very, very accountable for your work performance. How do you make accountability sticky for yourself? Here are two ideas:

- **Share the power.** Give a coach, mentor, or really strict friend the power to deny you something if you can't prove you kept your commitments. I have a fellow entrepreneur buddy I met when I lived in San Diego. He and a friend were trying to build their social media platforms, and they came up with a great accountability idea. Each month, they each sent $500 to a third party via Venmo. Then *after* they hit their monthly goal of social media posts—TikTok, Instagram, YouTube, and so on—and sent pictures as proof, they would get the money sent back to them. If one of them met the goal and the other didn't, the one who did would get the full $1,000. If neither of them did it, the third party kept the money. Because of the weight of the consequence, early on they each failed one time to hit their goals, but then they never missed another week. When you pay, you pay attention. Getting hit in the wallet is a huge consequence most people are very motivated to avoid.

- **Build around a deadline that's out of your control.** A class reunion, a cool group vacation, college tuition time—things you care about that happen at a set time that you don't determine—are pretty effective forms of "public accountability." The prospect of being embarrassed in front of your high school rivals, missing out on a cruise because you didn't have the deposit saved, or disappointing your child because you didn't have the tuition money are pretty strong motivators. These deadlines work because you can't move them back if you decide to get lazy. The deadlines are set, and you must act accordingly.

WHAT ABOUT REWARDS?

As I said, rewards are not as powerful as consequences because we fear pain more than we like pleasure, but if you know what your "reward trigger" is, they can be effective. A reward trigger is basically what you care about. Maybe you really, really care about beating your buddy at pickleball, winning your company sales bonus, getting time off from work, or something else that's important only to you. You can't rely on rewards entirely, but they can be part of your accountability mix, provided that you:

- **Plant small "teaser" rewards throughout your plan.** For example, when you keep your commitment for seven straight days, you earn a day off.

- **Bet on social approval and emotional encouragement.** They are more powerful than you think. For instance, the NBA's Golden State Warriors led the league in high fives and chest bumps during the years they won three out of four NBA championships. Clearly there was some powerful correlation between achievement and support from their teammates. Be sure to let your encouraging friends know what you're doing so they can provide some high-five encouragement.
- **Make sure your rewards don't set you back.** The reward for a week of great workouts shouldn't be a whole pizza. A tasty protein smoothie? Sure.
- **Reserve the big rewards for when you hit a substantial milestone.** A weekend away at a luxury Airbnb should be something you do after you pay off your $15,000 in credit card debt, not something you do after eating a healthy breakfast.

Remember, it's challenging to put in place accountability that you can't wiggle out of. Rely on friends, coaches, technology, and creativity. But please *do* put accountability systems in place, and make them ruthless. You'll thank them, and yourself, when you get awesome results.

MOMENTUM BUILDERS

NOW: Think of one way you can immediately raise the stakes for yourself with one of your personal goals. Can you sign up for a race or begin training for a physical challenge? Can you tell all your social media followers that your side hustle will officially be launching in sixty days? Pick one layer of external accountability that will immediately create a deeper investment for yourself.

TODAY: Explore some potential accountabilibuddies. If hiring a coach or mentor is not in the cards, think long and hard about who would fit the mold of someone you wouldn't want to disappoint or quit in front of. Schedule a call with that person and let them know why you are looking to talk with them. Make sure you aren't looking to take advantage of this person or receive free services of any kind. Remember, you are the one doing the work here; they are just one external layer of accountability to help you follow through.

YOUR GREATEST RETURN ON INVESTMENT

I had a client, Leah, who was planning to leave her job to go find something else when she ended up being offered the CEO job for her company. She was valued that much. But while she was excited and couldn't wait to accept it, there was something in her way. Leah confidently owned her decisions and was maybe considered bossy at times, but she was afraid of that side of her personality. She would make these gutsy calls and confront issues head-on, only to apologize and back down afterward to be sure she didn't step on any toes. That employee mentality doesn't work if you're going to be CEO or attempt to own or found your own thing.

When you're the leader, you've got to own the fact that not everybody's going to agree with you. Not everybody's going to like you, and to succeed, you must learn to be okay with that. When she hired me, it was the biggest investment she had ever made in coaching. We started immediately working on her owning her assertiveness and not being afraid of the consequences. Leah needed to adopt what I call a "CEO mentality" to succeed, not only in this new role but in her new pursuit of good to great. I kept reiterating that she had to take full ownership of her responsibilities and couldn't walk on eggshells if she was going to be CEO and do the job that she was being asked to do. The number one reason small business owners, founders, and C-level executives fail is that they attempt to run their business with the same mindset and approach they had when they were an employee.

Over the next few months, Leah started to step into a new level of confidence. Her fear went away. She didn't become callous or mean; she just made decisions that she believed were best for the company and then confidently stood by them. That even started to carry over into her personal life. She adopted this CEO mentality at home and in her health as well because if you're not the CEO in your own life, who the heck is? This mentality allowed Leah to run her first half-marathon and then a full marathon all within the first eight months of us working together, all while dominating in her new CEO role at work. Since then, Leah has now stepped away from being CEO of that company and is now running her own business—furthering the powerful idea of taking complete ownership over your life and future.

CALLING BULLSHIT

People hold on to some strange beliefs about letting things go. They convince themselves that all sorts of objects, habits, and so on are key to who they are, and they won't get rid of them even when those things hinder their progress as humans. That's just . . . what's the word? Stupid. Irrational thinking is the enemy of change. Any possession, habit, or relationship that obstructs you from fulfilling your potential doesn't belong in your life, period. Don't romanticize it. Lose it.

A DOWN PAYMENT IS REQUIRED

One of the most common dilemmas in coaching is knowing where to start. You sit across from someone like me in an office or on a Zoom call, and your whole life is laid out in front of you. There's your career, your company or business, and your personal life. Your fitness and your habits. Your finances and your mental health. Your dreams and biggest aspirations. Where do you start to get the changes you're looking for? What is the best way to invest your time and energy to get the most valuable results—the best ROI? Here's a way to cut through the confusion and make a great decision from the jump:

Your greatest ROI lies on the other side of the change you've most resisted.

It's true. I see it again and again. Clients will come to me and say, "Brett, I don't know what else to do. I've tried everything." Then we talk, and it turns out that's far from a fact and that there's a "no go" zone in their minds, something that they won't confront or even consider. Maybe it's a habit they're reluctant to change. Maybe it's a painful relationship they don't want to confront or a past failure they fear reliving. Not only have they not tried changing that *one thing*; they've also spent years bobbing and weaving to avoid facing it head-on.

If that's you, I *guarantee* that dealing with that bogeyman—that one part of your life you've been trying to avoid—will give you faster, more meaningful results than anything else you try on your path to change. When you do that, you not only prove to yourself that you haven't tried everything; you're also debunking that myth that change is impossible. It's your own uncomfortable truth that you need to come face-to-face with. You also prove to yourself that if you want something badly enough, you'll put on the gloves and step into the middle of the ring and say, "I'm ready to lean in and fight for this."

In investing, you want your ROI to be as high as possible, right? You'd love to invest $1,000 in a stock and have it be worth $10,000 in a year. Well, it's the same with high performance and personal transformation. Where's the pressure point? Where can you get the most bang for your buck? I actually have my own acronym for this: ROCI, pronounced "Rocky," like the boxer. It stands for "Return on *Courageous* Investment." It takes courage, Rocky-like guts, to confront that thing that you most want to avoid confronting. But that's where the big returns are.

Why? Because that habit, memory, pain, or relationship that you don't want to deal with is always hiding your biggest flaw or weakness. *Always*. That's why you don't want to go there. I've talked about how in my late twenties, drinking with my friends was a big part of my life. *Too* big. Nobody was better than me at motivating people to stay for one more drink or hit up one more bar. Anything to keep the fun going. I wanted to start tapping into my potential, but I also wanted to keep going out on the weekends and partying it up with my boys.

The two weren't compatible, and as uncomfortable as it was for me to admit, drinking and partying were excuses I used to avoid admitting I was unhappy with my life and having to pursue these big dreams that scared me. Drinking hurt my health, drained my money, sapped my will, ate up my time, and kept me looking forward to just two days of my week, but I was scared to know what my life would look like if I gave it up. Would I become lame? Lonely? A friendless recluse? What would it feel like not having a way to mask my emotions and unhappiness? What if I gave up drinking and *still* failed at starting my business and still struggled with money? Because of these fears, I fought, made excuses, and did everything I could to work around not giving up alcohol.

Then one day during an intense weekend training session, while gasping for air, hungover, and staring into a pool of my own sweat, I had an epiphany.

What if, instead of motivating people to have a *great night*, I could inspire them to have a *great life*?

Whoa! The idea felt huge but also weirdly attainable at the same time. Finally, I could clearly connect the dots and see why drinking and partying were holding me back from playing so much bigger and impacting so many more people. How could I inspire people to live a great life and unapologetically go after their dreams if I was stuck in the same comfort-seeking cycle they were? Once I admitted this, there was no avoiding it anymore. I knew I'd not only have to get uncomfortable, but I'd have to go first. So I forced myself to fill my weekend time with productive obligations and even started taking clients on Saturday and Sunday mornings, just so I'd have an excuse not to go out drinking. I know that may sound ridiculous, but the way I see it, it's not ridiculous if it works. This strategy worked for me until I gained the confidence to own my decision and tell my friends, "I'm not drinking."

You know what happened? I felt better. Actually, I felt awesome! My mind was clearer. Even though I was working weekends, because I wasn't hungover, I had more time to work out, go to conferences, and learn and read everything I could about coaching and speaking. For the first time in a long time, I was excited to wake up and get out of bed. With my new perspective, I saw that drinking and going out had been a social crutch. Who was I if I wasn't out at a bar with my friends? Now I knew. I was a speaker and a high-performance coach in the making. I didn't have to drink and could still have an identity. I was proud of who I saw when I looked in the mirror. In fact, I liked him *more*.

That's what I mean when I say that your biggest ROI is on the other side of what you don't want to confront. So let's confront it, you and me.

UNCOMFORTABLE TRUTH NO. 19

You might have to leave some people behind.

Throughout life, you will grow out of some relationships, romantic and otherwise. That's life. It happened to me. I couldn't stay in my hometown because many of my high school friends, whom I loved, wanted to do the same thing every week and weekend. I knew I wanted more. Leaving cost me some of those friendships, and it happened again when I moved away from the DC area eight years later. That will probably happen to you when you finally cross the bridge to the other side of what you've been avoiding. When you say, "No, this isn't for me anymore," some people hear, "I think I'm better than you." They take it personally, and if you take that to heart, it can stop you from doing what you need to do. So apply the *Good Will Hunting* solution. Will's the rebellious math genius, and at the end of the movie, he leaves his old life and hometown pals behind because he has a gift, and he owes it both to himself and to them not to waste it. Is it time for you to finally honor your gift?

KEEP THE CHANGE

This is most likely the hardest chapter to swallow so far, and it's only going to get harder. But you need to hear this. First off, you're terrified. You're afraid that if you take the leap—talk about what's wrong with your marriage, give up the foods you've loved since you were in third grade, sit down with a therapist and relive your childhood trauma—

that *nothing* will change. You won't get any ROI. You'll endure the pain, embarrassment, or cravings all for . . . nothing.

That's fair. But it's not going to happen. When you finally get to the other side of what you've been avoiding, two things always happen. First, you find out that confronting the thing you were avoiding wasn't as big, frightening, or hard as you thought. Clearing your house of unhealthy crap might not be fun, but after a week of not eating it, you feel a lot better and start seeing more *pros* instead of *cons*. Having "the talk" with your spouse is a lot less scary because—surprise—he or she really wanted to have it too. Talking with a therapist made you ugly cry, but it also gave you an incredible sense of peace and took a huge burden off your shoulders.

People do this and then say, "Why did I wait so long?" The other thing a lot of them say is, "Why was I making this such a big deal? I didn't want to give up pizza because my grandfather was Italian? Boy, that was silly."

The second thing that always happens is that you change. You really do become a new version of yourself when you find the courage to finally open that locked door—when you finally show up to Toastmasters or finally sign up for a dating app. I'm not saying you change overnight and everything's cool (there's still work to do), but something clicks. You're different. You're in control. The Wicked Witch is dead. You've stepped into your own CEO mindset, and any change becomes 100 percent possible.

So let's dig into some questions about this process that I think will help you get moving:

1. Is there something or someone you've been avoiding confronting, and does that avoidance coincide with the prolonged period you've been trying to make big, lasting changes but failing?

2. What's really stopping you?
3. What could potentially happen if you give up or confront what you've been dodging? Is there any potential fallout of making this change?
4. What will it continue to cost you if you *don't* make this change?

A TRADE WORTH MAKING

One of the other factors that keeps people stuck, missing out on that big ROI, is that they think the results of confronting the monster in the closet will be extreme. "If I give up drinking wine every Friday with my girlfriends, I can never have wine again, and my girlfriends will never hang out with me." "If I sign up for Bumble, the only way I'm ever going to meet somebody is on a dating app. I'm never going to be able to talk to anybody in a coffee shop again." Sounds exactly like my fears about giving up drinking, doesn't it?

It's easy to spiral into worst-case-scenario thinking. "If I stop drinking, I'm going to have no friends. I'll never enjoy another wedding or holiday, and I'll end up living alone in my mom's basement until I'm fifty." First of all, that's creepily specific. Stop that. Second, that's just your worst-case scenario and scarcity mindset talking. Nothing is irreversible, and making a big change like that doesn't turn your entire life upside down. It just lets a different side of you come out—usually, a better side. One that feels more aligned and confident. If you quit weekend binge drinking and never see those barhopping friends anymore, maybe you didn't have as much in common with them as you thought. Anybody who gets angered or triggered by your growth doesn't deserve your company. Your real friends want to see you happier, healthier, and better. So should your romantic partner, kids, colleagues, or boss.

I want you to try something. You've heard the term "devil's advocate." That's the voice in your head that whispers to you about all the worst-case scenarios in any situation. But nobody ever acknowledges the "angel's advocate." That's the ever-positive Jiminy Cricket on your shoulder that reminds you to think about all the best possible outcomes of any situation. So right now, let's play angel's advocate.

Look at that choice you've been ducking for years, that something you won't give up or confront because you're afraid of what happens when you do. Now imagine that you've confronted that demon or given up that temptation. What are three "best possible" outcomes that could come to pass? Write them down:

Angel's Advocate

What is the big change I'm confronting or deciding to remove?

____

Best possible outcome no. 1:

____

Best possible outcome no. 2:

____

Best possible outcome no. 3:

____

Remember a few chapters back when I said that you were only one or two big decisions away from changing everything? *Choosing to deal with the thing you've been trying so hard to avoid is one of those decisions.* Just doing this can unlock so much potential in your life because you're finally taking what was holding you back and pushing it out of the way, admitting to yourself that you're willing to trade good for the chance at great. Not only is that powerful, but that's also when you see real ROI.

What kind of ROI? That depends on you, what you confront or take back control over, and where you are in your process of change. But I find there are five grades of ROI:

1. You feel differently.
2. You think differently.
3. You act differently.
4. You see yourself differently.

And the last one is where real, lifelong change happens:

5. Your self-esteem, self-worth, values, and belief in what you're capable of all change for the better.

That's the toughest ROI to achieve and will take some time, but it's where the magic happens.

MOMENTUM BUILDERS

NOW: What have you been dodging for years that you should be confronting or creating a boundary with—a habit, a food, a person, a fear, something from your past? Just admitting this to yourself is a huge first step.

TODAY: Make your "angel's advocate" list. Write down the three or four best things that could happen when you get to the other side of that big thing. That's your ROI.

PART VI

WHAT'S YOUR NEXT UNCOMFORTABLE?

BLOOD, SWEAT, AND LAUGHTER

A few years ago, after my ruck marathon opened me up to endurance training, I did my first fifteen-mile trail run with my buddy Danny in the mountains near San Diego. At one point we just put our heads down and ran for twenty or thirty minutes and barely said a word to each other. We were huffing and puffing and sweat soaked through our shirts. As I was looking around at the breathtaking views from this mountain that nobody else was on, I knew this run was one of those experiences that would stay with me for a long time. With my ankles bloody because of scratches I'd gotten cutting through this area of sharp brambles, I started thinking about something.

All our best experiences, our best moments, the memories we remember forever—they all have something to do with pain, exhilaration, or fear. Those are the experiences that make us feel most alive.

Our fears were basic that day. What happens if we run out of water? What happens if one of us turns an ankle and we get stuck? I was thinking about this while I was running, and I came up with this acronym:

BESTLIFE. I thought it was pretty cool, and when we stopped to rest, I bounced it off my buddy. He was like, "Dude, that's not only pretty cool. It's accurate." That became one of the tools I use today when curating and evaluating experiences.

My BESTLIFE isn't the hashtag you see on social media when somebody really annoying shows you their perfectly decorated bedroom or the amazing meal they just cooked. My version is all about the experiences you have when you release the brakes on your life and go on that uncomfortable trek of changing your habits, confronting your demons, and leaving your old self behind. They're the experiences that draw blood, sometimes literally. The ones that force you to do what you've never done before. The ones that scare the shit out of you—that is, until you get past the fear and find yourself shouting with exhilaration and looking back with pride and accomplishment. Those are the experiences that tell you things are different, that you remember for life and become core memories, that evoke the emotions that make you feel really, truly alive.

This is what BESTLIFE really means:

- **Blood:** Yes, you will actually bleed sometimes. But blood really means that you're suffering in some way and that toughness and resilience are required. You're facing fears, confronting failures, sacrificing, and probably experiencing some pain—if not physical, then psychological. That's a reward because it lets you know that you're alive and that whatever is on the other side of that pain, you will have earned.
- **Exhilaration:** You'll feel excitement, ecstasy, and joy as you meet goals and do things you've never done before. This

comes with the rush of first-time experiences just as much as doing something old but in a new way.

- **Sweat:** You're going to work harder than ever, and you're going to enjoy the fruits of that labor—physically, mentally, emotionally, and financially. Think of this sweat equity as paying to unlock life's most epic experiences with hard work, elbow grease, and sacrifice.
- **Tears:** Your emotions will often be raw and powerful, and you'll be more connected to them than you've ever been in your life. You'll cry, laugh, and scream. Tears may come when you're at the top or when you're at the bottom, at the start, or at the finish. Whenever they come, they're a sign you're experiencing life's full spectrum of emotions.
- **Laughter:** Some of what you do—telling stories around a campfire, learning new skills, jumping in the pool with your clothes on, making a fool of yourself, or sneaking in somewhere you shouldn't be—will be hysterically fun. You'll be laughing so hard you can't breathe. Laughter is a sign that you feel accepted and safe and are having positive experiences with the people you are with.
- **Inspiration:** You'll inspire people who see that you're sticking to your plan and really making meaningful changes in your life. Some will want to emulate you and what they see as your extraordinary life. Some of the risks you take and experiences you embrace will even inspire *you.*
- **Fear:** Fear is a reward? Yes, because it's the thrillseeker's fear—the tingle in the spine as you stand in the open door of the plane, at the starting line, before you put in your two weeks' notice, or when you buy the plane tickets. It's fear

that humbles you while at the same time reminding you that you're in position to do great things.

- **Empathy:** You'll connect deeply with everyone else who's on a journey of change like you are. You will realize how grateful you are for this life and even find ways to share these same experiences with others.

CALLING BULLSHIT

Those #bestlife and #blessed hashtags on Instagram and Facebook aren't always what they seem. One of the good/bad things about social media is that people can curate their lives to look perfect to the public. That can make it seem like everybody but you has a gorgeous home, a six-pack, and a mountain of disposable income to travel around the world. They don't. Do your thing and don't worry about them. Learn to avoid comparing your chapter 1 with someone else's chapter 10 and your behind-the-scenes footage to someone else's highlight reel.

You earn your BESTLIFE by doing what I've described in previous chapters: honoring your contract with yourself, leaning into adversity, and making the choice to confront whatever you've spent the most time avoiding. Let me give you a couple of examples of what I mean.

I have a former client-turned-friend, Taylor, who's a wonderful violinist and even played at my wedding. She was one of my first personal training clients, as well as one of my first coaching guinea pigs. At one point she decided she wanted to take her fitness to the next level and train for something unique: the trapeze. What I love about Taylor is that she's willing to put herself in uncomfortable situations.

Well, less than a year later, after we started training specifically to get her upper body, grip, and core stronger for trapeze, she ended up performing on the trapeze at a local show. She enjoyed it so much and got so good she ended up being hired to play the violin *while on a trapeze* at this huge DC event! It was a ridiculously cool experience that she loved, and she would never have had it if she hadn't put herself out there to experience a full spectrum of BESTLIFE characteristics: lots of sweat and some physical pain, exhilaration, fear, lots of laughs, and so on.

Here's another. I had a client a while back, Frankie, who got in the best shape of her life at seventy and went on a hiking adventure with her husband and two friends. They hiked for hours each day, and when she got back, she told me she was so grateful for all the training work we had done because she felt like she was in better shape at seventy than when she was fifty. She was sending me photos from the tops of mountains that she had hiked up, and she told me, "All the other people my age, even some ten years younger, were looking up at us from the bottom of the mountain or taking the trolley to go up, and I didn't have to do that." She was proud of herself, in part because the experience had been hard. She had put in the work and sweat equity for months leading up to that trip, and that made it much more worthwhile. The reality is that Frankie is not common. Most seventy-year-olds won't have the opportunity to climb mountains because of health decisions they kept snoozing in their thirties, forties, and fifties.

BUILDING YOUR "OTHER" RÉSUMÉ

Those are *peak experiences*—moments of joy, insight, or even transcendence that raise your consciousness. They happen unexpectedly, usually when you're intensely engaged in a meaningful pursuit, feel a deep connection with people or nature, or are doing something beyond the boundaries of what you thought you were capable of. Peak experiences are transformative, leaving you with indelible memories and often inspiring personal growth or spiritual awakening.

Everybody is chasing peak experiences. They want those wonderful memories that they can share and point to as a moment when everything changed. Some people have them when they jump out of airplanes. Others have them when they travel and see a place they've dreamed about all their lives. Others have them when their kids are born or when they weep at a beautiful piece of music. But one thing all peak experiences have in common: they *do not* happen when you're wallowing in comfort. They don't happen while you're sitting on your couch with a remote in your hand or on your commute to the same old job.

Peak experiences are a reward exclusive to those willing to get uncomfortable.

A peak experience is part of the ROI you earn for embracing uncomfort. You get to live these extraordinary moments instead of just watching them online or seeing other people experience them. Instead of looking in the rearview mirror as you drive past the thing you've always said you wanted to do, all the greatest things in your life are still in the future. You're moving toward them.

Thinking this way is what allows you to start building what author, entrepreneur, and experience junkie Jesse Itzler calls your "life résumé." That's different from your professional résumé. You're building a life résumé of experiences and incredible moments and learning to reinvent yourself multiple times. The more you grow this list, the shorter your list of regrets becomes. You're building a photo album of memories you can point to and say, "*That's* who I am right there!" You're defining yourself, and when you've grown old and are sitting on the beach watching the sunset or sharing stories with your grandkids, you get the pleasure of looking back on all those memories and experiences and knowing that you really *lived*.

UNCOMFORTABLE TRUTH NO. 20

Pain is your friend.

Let's talk about pain because pain is really at the core of your BESTLIFE. I talk about pain as a positive thing, and it can be, but there are different kinds of pain, and you should know how to tell them apart. Beneficial pain is what I call "experiential pain," the discomfort or anxiety that comes from pushing your limits or trying something for the first time. Don't stress about that pain. Bad pain is called "warning pain," and you feel it when something's wrong. You're running with the wrong form, and you hurt your knee. You're in a new relationship that's abusive. You're investing in a company but fear that the founders are fraudulent. Don't ignore this kind of pain. If you're worried that something's wrong, investigate. Ask questions. If all is well, great. If not, get out before it's too late.

THE COST OF PEAK EXPERIENCES

Now you might look at my BESTLIFE list and see blood, sweat, tears, and fear and think, "Brett, what the hell are you getting me into? Am I actually going to be in pain?" Well, yeah, maybe. Some activities that lead to peak experiences could literally draw blood. You might get blisters while running the marathon you've wanted to run all your life. If you get in the best shape ever, you'll spend some time on the floor in a pool of perspiration, gasping for air, with fresh calluses on your hands. You're going to have those raw, cathartic moments when you're sitting around the fireplace and someone's telling a story that has you in tears. But you know what? The next minute, you and your friends are laughing so hard that your stomach hurts.

Pain, effort, and stress are part of uncomfort, and in that context, they're not bad. On that fifteen-mile run with Danny that I'll never forget, we really did run out of water, and it took every ounce of energy we had to make it back to the car, where we had extra water waiting for us. When we finally got to the car safely, we felt jubilation and euphoria. *We made it. I can't believe we just did that.* Fear was gone, and proud exhilaration took its place. The wide array of emotions is why that memory is still so vivid, and why we laugh about it every time we see each other.

There's a lame saying in the personal training world that goes, "Pain is weakness leaving the body." Nonsense. Pain, blood, fear—those are money. They're the cost of peak experiences, of living that BESTLIFE. There's another saying, "If it were easy, everybody would do it." Now that one I fully stand behind. Most people do everything they can to avoid the pain of uncomfort, not realizing all that does is prevent them from having peak experiences. When you're way out of your comfort zone, you should expect some pain, blood, sweat, and fear. When you see or feel them, greet them as friends! They're how you know you're on your way to something extraordinary and unforgettable—one step closer to reward and away from regret.

YOU WILL ALWAYS FIND WHAT YOU SEEK

There are still a few more uncomforts we will face on our journey together. But before we take the plunge into the last chapter, think about how you can seek out everything on the BESTLIFE list. During the next twelve months, I want you to *deliberately* seek out at least four experiences that you've never tried before or challenge yourself in areas where you think you're weak. One every ninety days.

If you're nervous speaking in front of a crowd, sign up for Toastmasters or join a networking group. If you feel self-conscious because you don't know anything about opera or the theater, subscribe to your city's opera company season. If you're out of shape, join a running group training for their first 5K. If you're shy about meeting people, sign up for a dating app. Do you suck in the kitchen? Register for a cooking class.

You get the picture. Who you have to become to complete these challenges will have a ripple effect on the rest of your year. Sure, you might white-knuckle your way through some early dates or networking events. You might feel silly attending a cooking class with a bunch of strangers. But you won't die, and you'll be deep in uncomfort territory, where unique, memorable experiences happen.

Once you realize you can confront the blood, sweat, and fear that come with these challenges, you'll feel more confident and ready to chase peak experiences such as training for a marathon, trekking into the Himalayas, starting a business, or having kids.

One tip as you head in that direction, though: *Practice mindfulness*. While you're having these uncomfortable, extraordinary, unforgettable experiences, be in the moment. Every now and then, stop what you're doing and take a beat to look around at what you're doing and whom you're doing it with. Don't be in such a rush to get back to the car and bandage up your bloody ankles that you forget to enjoy the breathtaking view of running in the mountains. Savor the fact that you're alive in the moment. It's in these moments you'll connect to your deepest sense of fulfillment. Living an extraordinary life is its own reward.

To quote one of my favorite childhood movie characters and life résumé legends, Ferris Bueller, "Life moves pretty fast. If you don't stop and look around once in a while, you could miss it."

MOMENTUM BUILDERS

NOW: Make a list of some of the peak experiences you'd like to add to your "life résumé" in the next few years—travel, career, physical accomplishment or races, creativity, marriage and kids, whatever. Don't limit or restrict yourself.

TODAY: Now figure out four experiences that you've never tried before or that challenge you. What are they? Where can you find them? What will they cost? How can you get the time off? Some may take a weekend and a whole lot of training, while some can be accomplished in a few hours. Choose and plan accordingly, get them scheduled on your calendar, and *get excited*!

GET UNCOMFORTABLE BEING COMFORTABLE

And just like that, we've come full circle. We've gone from the idea of uncomfort, through all the ways we sabotage our own progress, debunked myths about things such as willpower and motivation, run the Sunday Setup program, and figured out how not to renegotiate contracts with ourselves or snooze our precious time away. Now it's time to go out into the world and put all that into action. But first, a quick story.

Once, a king received two hawks as a gift and assigned the royal falconer to train the beautiful birds. Before long, the falconer entered the king's chambers, bowed low, and announced that he had a report on the hawks' progress. One bird was soaring high on the thermals, but the other bird just sat on its branch and looked around.

Frustrated, the king brought in his gamekeeper to try to get the second hawk to fly, to no avail. Next, supposed magicians from across the kingdom appeared at court, each claiming he could get the hawk airborne. None succeeded. Finally, the king thought to send for a local hunter, someone who knew the area's wildlife. A nearby hunter was found and brought to the palace, and the falconer explained the problem. Within an hour, the king looked out his window and was thrilled to see the second hawk flying high next to its companion. He had the hunter brought to him immediately.

"How did you accomplish this?" asked the king.

The hunter bowed. "Sire, I simply cut the branch the bird had been sitting on."

We're all prone to getting too comfortable, and that's true even after we've taken huge strides into the unknown, faced challenges, and become best friends with uncomfort. The temptation is to tackle something huge and life changing, achieve it, then sit back, congratulate ourselves, and say, "Well, that's that."

But uncomfort is a life sentence. As soon as you think you're close to being your highest self and have no more changes to make, you get humbled by someone or something. Growth never stops. Seeking uncomfort is a lifelong pursuit.

I want you to become uncomfortable about getting too comfortable.

When you achieve your long-term vision—when you've reached your first fitness goal, gotten your business off the ground and made it sustainable, found the right life partner—you should absolutely take a victory lap. Take two! Celebrate, savor the progress, reflect on the pain and sacrifice, and enjoy every moment. But do not sit back and become complacent, thinking that's the end of your journey. Don't let your motto become, "Back in the day, I used to . . ." Like this book, life has multiple chapters and phases, and you can reinvent yourself at any time. Become someone who gets restless after too much comfort and success. Who starts asking, "How can I challenge myself in a new way? How can I make a difference? How can I continue to grow and experience new levels of life?" Someone who starts looking for new sources of uncomfort.

That's how the greats become great. They never stop growing and pushing themselves. The late Kobe Bryant came into the NBA as a seventeen-year-old phenomenon, but he wasn't a great outside shooter. So he made himself into one through endless work, often in the wee hours when everyone else was asleep. He referred to this in a 2016 speech accepting an Icon Award from ESPN:

> *We're not on this stage just because of talent or ability. . .*
>
> *We're up here because we had a dream and let nothing stand in our way.*
>
> *If anything tried to bring us down, we used it to make us stronger.*
>
> *We were never satisfied, never finished. We will never be retired.*[*]

Man, if that doesn't give you goose bumps . . .

That's the mentality I want you to have as we reach the end of this book and the beginning of your personal journey. Don't ever be satisfied. Become distrustful of too much comfort, too much satisfaction. In truth, I don't think this will be a problem. See, when you reach your goal and become comfortable with uncomfort, you won't be the same person you were when you started out. What was uncomfortable a year ago or five years ago won't be uncomfortable anymore. You'll have to look for some new uncomfort so you can keep growing and evolving.

---

* Bryant, Kobe. Review of Acceptance Speech, ESPN Icon Award. Presented at the 2016 ESPY Awards. Accessed July 13, 2016. https://www.youtube.com/watch?v=HArU4KGO7DA.

How can you possibly know if you're getting too comfortable? There's actually a pretty reliable way. If you go, say, a year without learning new skills and experiencing the kind of emotions I talked about in the BESTLIFE chapter—joy, exaltation, exhilaration, free-fall terror, gut-busting laughter, overwhelming love—then there's a good chance you've fallen back into a rut. That's when it's time to step up, step out, find a new goal, build a new Sunday Setup, crack your knuckles, and get back to work.

Throughout this book, I've tried to give you some brutally honest tough love with a big bear hug at the end. I've killed some comfortable myths and forced you to face some uncomfortable truths, but I've tried my best to do it in an empowering way, with a few dad jokes and f-bombs thrown in for a laugh. As we come to the close, let's do that again. Here's some wisdom to take with you:

- **Stay humble and curious.** You're never going to know everything, even about the subjects in which you feel like an expert. Even as I finish this book, I may be great in some areas yet also still a complete beginner and first-time author. Embrace those opportunities.
- **Check your self-delusion.** Be careful you're not lying to yourself about things. It's very intoxicating to do so, and people who accept their own bullshit are the ones who become the most complacent.
- **Believe in yourself.** If you don't believe you can win, you never will. Anyone who ever did anything great, first believed it was possible. Adopt the "beginner's mindset" about everything new and embrace your imposter syndrome like a badge of honor.
- **Define your own success.** The key is to chase meaningful goals that matter to you. You must not confuse healthy

growth with a never-ending pursuit of accumulation, external validation, and chasing someone else's definition of success. That road will never lead to peace or fulfillment. Make sure you are playing and attempting to win the right game.

Remember, the goal here is to build the best version of the person you are today, and that doesn't happen overnight. Everything great in your life will come from growth and challenging yourself again, and again, and again. Here's the process for doing that:

1. When you finally hit your big goal, savor your success. Rest, reward yourself, share your story, and look back to see whom you can extend a helping hand to.
2. When you start to feel restless (and you will), start looking for your next uncomfort. What other part of yourself could you improve on? What longtime goal is still out of reach? What haven't you confronted yet?
3. Set your broad goal, then map out the sacrifices and changes involved in reaching it. Remember, a year is a long game made up of a lot of short games. You must win mornings, days, and weeks to win months and years.
4. Make your ninety-day plan, including consequences and rewards.
5. Prepare your first Sunday Setup and embrace this process as your weekly self-accountability checkpoint.
6. Start enjoying the uncomfort. Lean on the tools and self-knowledge you gained the first time around.
7. When you reach your next goal, rinse and reuse the processes, strategies, and momentum-building steps you learned here.

8. Keep this book in your back pocket and reread it anytime you feel yourself slipping into comfort or when you need some clarity around the uncomfortable decisions you may be avoiding. You can apply this book to each and every phase of life you encounter. Be sure to leverage it to your advantage.

I don't want you to lead a life of nothing but uncomfort, but I do want you to explore growth and self-discovery and to reap the rewards. Anyone can live an extraordinary life of true alignment and fulfillment, and there are people all around you doing it, in books, on TV, on social media, in your town, and right in front of you. They're not special and don't have anything you don't have. They're just willing to do what most people aren't: get clear on their process and plan, stay consistent and disciplined, and have enough belief and courage to begin.

Well, now *you* have a process and a plan, and hopefully through the lessons and actions you've already taken in this book, you've created the belief that it's possible for you too.

There's a world of knowledge out there, but all the knowledge in the world isn't going to change you. Reading, making lists, speaking affirmations—that won't get it done. It's time to find your uncomfort and take it down. If you fuck up, so what? You try again: 30 percent action is better than 100 percent wishful thinking. An imperfect something is always better than a perfect nothing. Ms. Frizzle would call that "messy action." If you fail the first time to confront your fear or change a bad habit, you're still farther ahead than you would be if you were sitting on your butt doing nothing.

Remember when I said you were one or two decisions away from changing everything? Confronting the thing you've been working hard to avoid is the second big choice. Reading this book is the first one. Now that you've read it, you don't need to jump to the next personal growth book. You don't need another diet. You don't need another workout program. You don't need to follow another social media account. You don't need more knowledge. You just need to shut out the noise, and you need to *take action*. Find that thing you've been avoiding, lean the hell in, and face it. Build up momentum. Build your plan and follow it. Embrace the suck. Face the fear. Never get complacent.

That's one pivotal choice down. The next one is up to you. You've got this. I'm absolutely sure of it. You're ready to get started. You've been ready, and I can't wait to see what you'll do next.

Your coach,
Brett Eaton

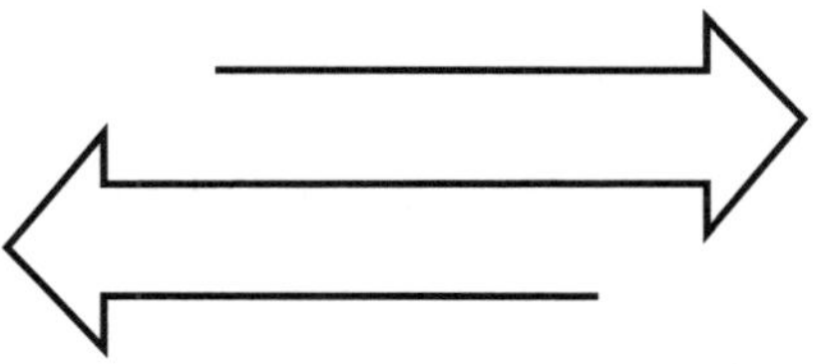

ACKNOWLEDGMENTS

Wow, how do I even begin to thank all of the people who have supported me, encouraged me, coached me, guided me, and helped mold me into the person I am today? There is no way I have enough space or words to properly express my gratitude and acknowledge all of the family, friends, coaches, colleagues, mentors, and idols that I want to thank. But I will try.

Thank you to my amazing and beautiful wife, Anne. I'm forever thankful every day for the love, joy, and laughter you've brought into my life. Thank you for all the support during the long hours and understanding of the late nights in the office when I just couldn't stop writing. Lastly, thank you for the helpful feedback and suggestions for this book, even though I wouldn't let you read it until it was finished. I love you, baby.

Thank you to my parents for being my heroes.

Thank you, Dad, for reminding me that being the richest man in town has nothing to do with money and everything to do with how you treat people. You were the best dad a young man could ask for. You taught me to be obsessive with my word and my goals and also to enjoy life and not take myself too seriously. To be a winner and not a whiner. Thank you for everything you taught me during our time together, everything you taught me since you've been gone, and—above all else—that people will never forget how you made them feel. I love you, Dad.

Mom—thank you for always encouraging me to be a dreamer and for your endless support of my crazy ideas. You're the strongest, kindest, and most selfless and resilient woman I've ever met, and all of my big-hearted traits come from you. You've always been my biggest fan, and that's all a kid could really ask for. Thanks for never letting me leave the house without first reminding me to "never forget who you are." I hope this book is proof that I've never forgotten. Hugs and hand pounds. I love you, Mom.

Thank you, Beez, for being an amazing stepfather and for all the love you've provided our family all these years. Thank you for always being there and for teaching me so many things my dad never got the chance to. You're the biggest reader I know, and while you only enjoy fiction, I hope you'll give this one a read.

To the most influential coaches and teachers I had growing up—Jackie Regina, Coach Briggs, Coach Vogt, Coach Ragasa, and Mr. Conklin: You all taught me invaluable lessons about life and impacted me more than you could ever know. You showed me what putting in the work truly means and emphasized the importance of taking full responsibility for every situation. These lessons have helped me become the leader I always aspired to be. Thank you for guiding me through the hardest year of my life, for pulling me back when I started down the wrong path, and for not giving up on me—even when I may have given you reasons to.

Thank you to all my business coaches, therapists, accountabilibuddies, and mentors—there are too many of you to name, but if you think this might be you, it is. Thank you for believing in me, encouraging me to play big, showing me the way, and setting the bar high.

Thank you, Lewis Howes, for introducing me to personal growth through your podcast and your live Summit event, which have both been massively influential in my life. You were a mentor to me long before we ever met. That moment you invited me to step onto your stage with you is one I will always remember. Thank you for creating a place for dreamers like me to feel normal, feel seen, and see what's possible when we commit to chasing greatness. I can't thank you enough for your endorsement of this book.

Thank you, Jen Gottlieb, for leading the way and showing me what is possible with relentless effort, speaking your goals into existence, and doing the work. You have always put people first, and I respect and appreciate you more than you know. We've sure come a long way since lunch at our first SOG. Thank you so much for your kind words about this book. I'm forever grateful to you.

Thank you, Sterling Hawkins, for your friendship and mentorship, as well as for the amazing stories we shared while hiking for twenty hours straight. I'm grateful to you and very much appreciate your guidance, wisdom, and support for both my speaking career and this book.

Thank you to Tim Vandehey for being in the foxhole with me all these months and helping me bring this book to life. I appreciate your willingness to take risks with this book and believe in my unorthodox ideas—and even have some of your own. There is no way this book sees the light of day without your help and without you pushing me. You are a true pro, my friend.

Thank you, Naren, Brandon, and the Amplify Team, for believing in this book and fulfilling a young man's dream of being a published author. You guys are all pros and have made this long process fun, rewarding, and enjoyable.

Thank you to all the friends, teachers, bosses, and people who believed in me, as well as the ones who doubted me. Thank you for challenging me to fight for what I wanted to become, as well as reminding me what I wanted to avoid. I couldn't have done this without you, and you each have left a mark that I am grateful for.

Thank you to the many people who shared ideas, read early drafts of the manuscript, and provided testimonials, feedback, coaching, support, and friendship. I appreciate you.

Thank you to all my past and current clients, gym and studio members, and colleagues for putting your trust in me and allowing me to be your coach as well as grow alongside you. I'm grateful for your belief in me, your willingness to do the work, and the valuable lifelong lessons that I learned from you that I'm now able to share with the world. You all inspire me so much, and this book is a testament to all of you who have ever been #MotivatedByBrett.

And lastly, thank you to *you* for reading this book. I cannot express how grateful I am for you. You're the reason I wrote this book. All of the stories, strategies, and tough love in this book are in service of helping you see what's possible when you lean into uncomfort and stop allowing pain and excuses to run your life.

For those feeling stuck, currently struggling, or at a crossroads in life, I hope reading this book has shown you that you're not alone. I've been right where you are. I hope this book makes you feel seen and gives you the encouragement to boldly do what most people are unwilling to do, and take the path less traveled. You're not stuck—you just need to make a bold decision. Take the risk, lean in, and stop playing by someone else's rules. Make your own rules. You have a gift, a purpose, and can have it all if you are willing to face the fear and go toe-to-toe with uncomfort.

Regardless of how this book transforms your life, I'd love for you to give a copy to a friend or someone you know who needs this message. Start your own positive ripple effect by sharing this helpful resource and inspiring someone through your own actions. I truly believe you are meant for more. I hope you believe that as well. The blueprint is right here in this book. Don't waste it. It's time for you to embrace the fact that life is going to be *Uncomfortable Either Way*, so why not choose the one that comes with rewards?

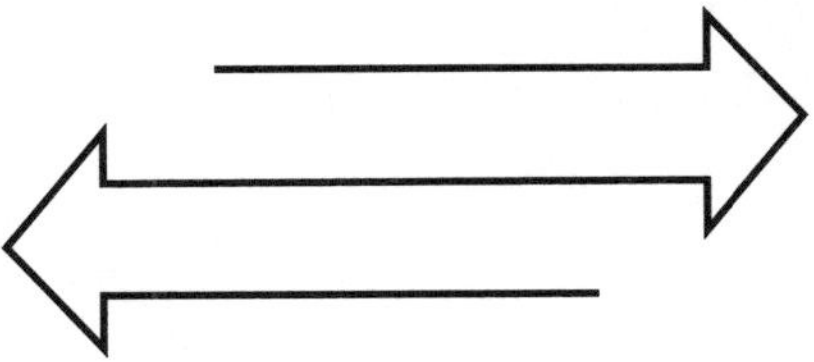

ABOUT THE AUTHOR

BRETT EATON is a sought-after keynote speaker and high-performance coach. Over the past seventeen years, Brett has collaborated with top performers in a variety of industries to develop unique methodologies and a personalized approach that have helped hundreds of audiences, companies, and clients make the bold decisions that have allowed them to reach thousands of personally fulfilling goals, start more than two hundred businesses, generate millions of dollars in revenue, and unlock newfound standards and fulfillment in their lives.

Brett doesn't just speak about high performance and the importance of embracing the uncomfortable—he lives and breathes it. When he's not on stage inspiring, Brett can be found competing out on the beach volleyball courts with his wife or training for his next physical challenge. Brett has rock-climbed up Mount Washington, completed a solo marathon wearing a twenty-five-pound weighted vest, and hiked twenty-seven miles and accumulated 29,029 feet of elevation in thirty-six hours, and for the past four years, he's completed 911 burpees on September 11 to honor the victims of 9/11. Brett doesn't just inspire through his words. He's a man on a mission to seek out the uncomfortable and maximize fulfillment.

He currently lives in Florida with his wife, successful entrepreneur Anne Mahlum.